LEGENDS & LORE
OF
SOUTHWEST VIRGINIA

LEGENDS & LORE
OF
SOUTHWEST VIRGINIA

SHANE S. SIMMONS AND MELODY BLACKWELL-WEST

THE
History
PRESS

Published by The History Press
Charleston, SC
www.historypress.com

First published 2023

Manufactured in the United States

ISBN 9781467155045

Library of Congress Control Number: 2023938428

Melody: To my Momma Jewel, for all your love and support. And to Eli Dye, the next Blackwell historian.

Shane: To Kennedy, Sean and Will, with all my love.

CONTENTS

ACKNOWLEDGEMENTS

We discovered that writing about our home area is a deeply personal endeavor and a true labor of love to present the stories of the people and places we've long called home. It is of the utmost importance to us that we present these tales in an honest and respectful way. We want to thank everyone who helped assist in writing this book in all ways, great and small. Thanks to several folks who were so gracious in assisting us, we gained a deeper understanding of some stories we knew and, in some cases, brand-new stories we weren't familiar with previously. A special thanks to Kate Jenkins with The History Press for all her wonderful guidance and patience in the writing process. We also would like to thank our YouTube followers of our Real Appalachia and Real Shane and Melody channels for encouraging us to continue our work in preserving these stories. We attempted to include the best stories from the widest array of areas to give as full of a picture as possible of a region that is incredibly diverse.

We would have never been able to complete this book without the generous financial support of our donors and from our patrons from Patreon.com. Thank you to these patrons:

Bradly Fitzpatrick
Jan Trent
Donald Nowve
Dana Richards
Melissa Chandler-Farleigh
Dean Kirkner

Leland Morris
MattyB83
David and Judy Winton
Nathan Keesecker
Michael Rudnick
Stephen G Morris

ACKNOWLEDGEMENTS

Penny Wright
Glenn Farnham
Jarrod Mitchell
Spooky Appalachia
Jimmy Smith
Jennifer Timmons
Joe Grassi
Uncle Ben
Holly Willis
Mia
John Perdue
Rene Tetron
Tiffany Carlson
Julian Frasier
Carol Simmons Smith
William Martin
Ronald Tirrachia
Tracy Bosier
Tabitha Buckles
Joey Snider
Pam Broderick
Madhu Kollu
Susan Burrows-Rangel
James Lagan
Eric Peck
George Sawtooth
Gregory Lewis
Keith and Donna Timmons
Chris Jurkowski

Rob Crotts
Christian Williams
Ghyontonda Mota
David L. Mullins
Joe Sullivan
Audrey Welch
Angela Smith
Andrew DeLong
Matthew Coon
Steve Surber
Wayne Maynard
Brian Serway
Jessica Rodrigues
George McNair
Bill Whitworth
Mike Adams
Shawn Hannah
Brad and Angela Davis
Michael Genecki
Kara Wyatt Rasnake
Jonathan Gartland
Karen Caddle
Andrew Diseker
Carol Wilder
Kimberly Carr
Dee Simmons Alban
Bill Seward
Daniel Armstrong
Anna Long

Thanks to these wonderful donors:

Bradly Fitzpatrick
Don and Debbie Adams
Jim Maiden
Sherri Ganske
Dana Richards
Charles Smith

Dean Kirkner
HS Serry
Denis Frauenhofer
David Hurst
Michael Cantrell
Richard Sitler

ACKNOWLEDGEMENTS

Brian Robinson
Sara Bella
Vern Weller
Earl Spratley
Steve from SC
Brenda Bray
Christopher Branham
James Gould
Steve Beatrice
Brenda Lane
Boyd Breece
Charlie Smith
Chelsea M. Jackson
Nancy G Brooks
Shelly Fenley
Brian Robinson
Betty Antoine
Christopher Moore
Kathleen Burnett
David McCray
David House
Randy and Dena Key
John Neilson
R. Parks Lanier Jr.
Larry Allen

Ryan Farmer
Iris Lee Underwood
Vicki Murphy
Virginia Martin
Anne Wagner
Jim Peck
Heather Lovasz
Patti Dibble
Christopher Moore
Mark P. Gholson
Teresa Dalton
AJ Wallace
Josh Taylor
Barbara Awbrey
William Mills
Robert Morgan
Chris Coleman
Chelsea Jackson
Logic Milkbone
Dana Lynch
Robert Hill
Jerry Murphy
Savannah Johns
Toni Johns

MELODY

I want to thank my "Momma," Jewel Blackwell, first and foremost. I have beautiful childhood memories of my mom taking me to the library to pick out books and reading me stories every night, funny voices for each character and all. She has always cultivated a love of reading and books for me, which also developed into a love of writing. I have always felt so loved and supported, and for that and so much more, I am forever grateful.

I also want to thank my dad, Jerry Dye; my sister, Tiffany Onate; and my brother, Heath Dye. I appreciate all your love and support. I'm also so grateful to get to be an aunt to the best niece and nephews any woman could ask for. Cameron Dye, Cristian Onate, Emery Onate and Lucas Dye have been four of my greatest blessings in life.

My aunt and uncle Jeni and Eddie Neely deserve a huge thank-you for the tremendous love and support they've shown me throughout my life. To my uncles in Heaven, Rod and Lonnie Blackwell, I am also forever grateful: Rod, for being a wealth of information of history and folklore, and Lonnie for being the best storyteller I've ever known in my life. I am eternally grateful for my family who have made me who I am.

Susan "Susie" Fields-Chandler, I am so grateful for the new friendship and all the information and tales she so graciously shared with me about her beloved Papaw Charlie "Cedar Creek Charlie." And to Russell County Public Library for helping me with their vast collection of local history.

SHANE

I am grateful for my children, Kennedy, Sean and Will Simmons, for being my constant motivation and inspiration to keep moving forward in life. They are constant reminders of all that is good in life. Thanks to my parents, Bill and Linda Simmons, for raising me in this beloved Southwest Virginia where I have called home the majority of my life. Growing up in the tiny community of Doran, just outside the town of Richlands, exposed me to many of the tales in this book and gave me an appreciation for the rich history of these hardworking people that make Southwest Virginia home.

Family has impacted me in so many ways and has inevitably made its way into the book. My brothers Billy and Ben Simmons and cousins John and Matt Simmons spent a lot of time exploring the hills and hollers of Southwest Virginia. Hopefully, my nephews Logan and Vince Simmons will carry on some of the history and traditions of the area.

INTRODUCTION

Nestled in the Appalachian Mountains, Southwest Virginia is a region steeped in rich history, folklore and tradition as deep as any holler and as rich as the coal seams that fill these mountains with the "black diamond." From the earliest Native American settlements to the Scots-Irish pioneers who carved out a living in the rugged terrain, this area has always been home to a unique and diverse group of people. The European immigrants and African Americans from the Deep South who were recruited to work in the coal mines made this part of the United States a true representation of the "Great American Melting Pot."

Throughout the centuries, these communities have developed their own legends and lore, passed down from generation to generation. Some of these tales are based in reality, while others are pure fantasy, but all of them serve as a testament to the resilience and creativity of the people who call this place home.

In *Legends and Lore of Southwest Virginia*, we explore some of the most fascinating stories and characters from the region's past. From the ghostly haunts of the Octagon House and the Major Graham Mansion to the larger-than-life exploits of legendary people from Francis Gary Powers to Molly Tynes, these tales bring the history and culture of Southwest Virginia to life in a way that is both captivating and unforgettable.

Whether you are a native of the area or a curious outsider, *Legends and Lore of Southwest Virginia* offers a window into the past and an appreciation for the enduring spirit of the people who have shaped this region. So come along on this journey through time and discover the legends and lore that make Southwest Virginia a truly one-of-a-kind place.

I

LEGENDARY PEOPLE
OF SOUTHWEST VIRGINIA

THE CARTER FAMILY:
THE FIRST FAMILY OF COUNTRY MUSIC

In the early 1900s in Southwest Virginia, times were hard, and comfort was needed. Two sources of comfort that sometimes intermingled were faith and music. These two things were relied on heavily by the Carter Family, whom many credit as the forerunners of the country music industry. Hailing from the green hills of Scott County, the trio walked into a recording studio in Bristol, Virginia, on August 1, 1927, and made history in what now is known as "The Bristol Sessions."

Alvin Pleasant "A.P." Carter (also known as "Doc") knew exactly who Sara Dougherty was, but it wasn't until he heard her singing that he truly noticed her. It was then that their courtship began, and the couple was married in June 1915. A.P. worked various jobs as a salesman, a blacksmith and a carpenter while Sara tended the small farm at their Scott County cabin, but the couple's real passion was making music together. They often sang in churches and for small audiences for money, but never enough to make a living. They especially enjoyed playing for friends and family, including Sara's first cousin Maybelle Addington.

Maybelle was only six years old at the time of A.P. and Sara's marriage, but she was always the most excited to dance along to their music. She would sometimes ask to join in singing with the couple. As Maybelle got older, she became quite the musician herself, excelling on the banjo, autoharp and guitar. Maybelle became known for her talents, especially with the autoharp, throughout Scott County by the age of twelve. It was her talent with the guitar, however, that made history. Maybelle pioneered a guitar method in which she thumb-picked the melody on the lower strings while the other fingers strummed the rhythm from the upper strings in a style that had never been done before.

In 1922, Maybelle's family moved from Copper Creek in Russell County to Bristol, which put them closer to A.P. and Sara. It was at this time the three began making music together almost daily. It also made the later courtship between Maybelle and A.P.'s younger brother, Ezra "E.J.," easier. In 1926, E.J. and Maybelle married in Bristol. A.P., Sara and Maybelle continued making music together and separately around Scott County, often to Sara's discontent.

A.P. was convinced there was money to be made as a musical career, but the ladies of the group were not convinced. Sara also had moral reservations about playing spiritual music for money, but A.P. pressed on. One day while visiting Cecil McClister's record store, as he often did when in Bristol, A.P. was told of a representative from Brunswick Record Company being in the area looking for new country music acts. Cecil helped his friend work out a deal to record their singing for twenty-five dollars, but there were some issues. Maybelle was in Roanoke at the time with E.J. for his work on the railroad, and Sara was not enthused. The years of traveling to perform, along with a house to keep and three children to care for, were weighing on her. It was the twenty-five dollars that she could not pass up.

Unfortunately, without Maybelle's impressive guitar strumming, A.P. and Sara fell flat, and their record was not made for contract. A.P. was discouraged and gave in to his wife's wishes to slow down their musical adventures. Luckily, when a man from Victor Records came around to Bristol, his friend Cecil at the record store was able to convince him to give it another go. The community loved the music of the Carter Family, and Cecil knew they had what it took to make it. The date was set for August 1, 1927, for the trio to meet with Ralph Peer, the representative for Victor Records.

Opposite: Marker for the Bristol Sessions off State Street in Bristol, Virginia. *Melody Blackwell-West.*

Above: Boyhood home of A.P. Carter, restored and moved a short distance from the Carter Family Fold. *Melody Blackwell-West.*

The Carter Family met with Peer that day above Cecil McClister's record store. They first sang for him "Weeping Willow," which was based on Psalm 137:2. Sara's voice enchanted Peer just as it had A.P. all those years before. A very pregnant Maybelle blew him away on the guitar. Their sound was exactly what he was looking for. They spent the rest of the day singing for him, just as Jimmie Rodgers had the day before and as he would the day after. A contract was signed that day, but nothing seemed to change afterward for the Carter Family. There were more requests for appearances, but no new money was coming in for them. They had no idea the impact they had just made in the Bristol Sessions.

It wasn't until about a month later when A.P. took another trip to Bristol that his friend Cecil handed him the first Carter Family record sent by Peer along with a letter describing the success of their new hits. The little store in Bristol had completely sold out all two hundred copies they were sent, and the Atlanta area sold two thousand. Despite the boom in sales, money was still a problem for the family. As they received only a quarter of a cent

The original Carter Family. A.P. and Sara standing, Maybelle sitting. *Wikimedia Commons. Carter Family promotional portrait by the Victor Talking Company*.

from all sales at that time, the $150 they were sent was tremendously helpful in paying off debts, but it didn't last long. The Depression had hit Virginia hard, and A.P. went north again for work.

It was during his time in Detroit that he worked alongside many men of color, mostly from the Deep South, who also relied heavily on music. A.P. was struck by the heart-wrenching loneliness of their songs and took great influence from Black culture after that experience. Thankfully, his days of hard labor were soon to be behind him. While in Detroit, Sara received a letter and $100 from Peer asking the Carter Family to come to New Jersey to make more records. Then in May 1928, several more songs were recorded, including a live audience favorite, "Keep on the Sunny Side" (the sunny side being the light of God's wisdom). This new recording session officially made them career musicians.

While their record sales were in the millions, not much income came from royalties. The bulk of their income came from live performances, which was tricky at times due to Maybelle and E.J.'s moves to Bluefield and later Washington, D.C., due to his work with the railroad, but the group managed. As their popularity grew, so did their touring. A.P. booked more and more tour dates farther from home, to the women's displeasure. The balance of performing, recording, keeping up a home and tending to children proved to be too much. In 1933, A.P. and Sara separated but continued to perform as a group after a short break. Sara and Maybelle demanded less touring, however, which fortunately kept the group together longer.

In 1935, they signed a new contract with American Record Corporation, and by 1937 they were as popular as ever, getting a great deal to sing on the radio out of a station in Texas. After a while, their children started performing along with them. Maybelle's daughters Helen and Anita became radio fan favorites, while her middle daughter, June, struggled to keep up vocally. Maybelle started teaching June the autoharp at age ten in order to keep her place in performances. June's personality also drew attention. A.P. saw a special quality in June and encouraged her to introduce more comedy into the show. A.P. and Sara's daughter Janette sang as a soloist on the radio program as well. A new Carter Family was evolving.

The original Carter Family was given an impressive new radio contract out of Charlotte, North Carolina, in 1941. Sara had remarried a cousin of A.P.'s, Coy Bayes, in 1939 and had since spent a great deal of her time in California, where her new husband had made a life in the timber business. To A.P. and Maybelle's surprise, Sara also agreed to the radio program, but this would be the last stint of the original Carter Family trio.

Road signs in Hiltons, Virginia, honoring AP Carter and the popular Carter Family song "Wildwood Flower." *Melody Blackwell-West.*

A.P. moved back to his cabin in Scott County and established a general store. Sara lived out her remaining days in California with her second husband. It was Maybelle and her daughters who continued performing. Eventually, the Carter Family became the Carter Sisters, with June being the standout due to her vibrant personality. After a short tour with Elvis Presley, Elvis suggested Johnny Cash hire June as part of his troupe. June was credited as a co-writer for Johnny's hit songs "The Matador" and "Ring of Fire," but their chemistry onstage and off was where the real magic was. In 1968, Johnny and June were married and became one of the most admired couples in American music history.

In 1970, Sara and Maybelle reunited along with Johnny Cash's troupe for a night of recognition of the Carter Family and Jimmie Rodgers as pioneers of country music by the Country Music Hall of Fame in Nashville. Johnny Cash was the one to pay respects to A.P., who had passed away peacefully in his Scott County home in 1960. Although the record store along State Street in Bristol where the magic of the now famous Bristol Sessions occurred has long since been replaced by a parking lot, A.P. and Sara's daughter Janette made sure the old family homestead stayed preserved.

Left: Vintage sign for Old Time Music at the Carter Family Fold. *Melody Blackwell-West.*

Right: Sign honoring A.P., Sara and Maybelle on the side of the Carter Family Fold. *Melody Blackwell-West.*

In 1974, the Carter Family Fold in Hiltons, Virginia, was established. Janette had promised her father on his deathbed that she would make sure the legacy he created would live on. She created a family environment in the form of a music hall in which she hosted music lovers from all over for thirty years until her passing in 2006. The venue was even the scene of Johnny Cash's last live performance before his death in 2003.

Today, the Carter Family Fold is managed by Janette's daughter, Rita Forrester.

The Carter Family created a legacy that put Bristol on the map as the "Birthplace of Country Music." But they also changed the course of music entirely by bringing the hillbilly music of Southwest Virginia to the entire nation and eventually the world. The sweet sound they brought showed the strong faith and undying hope of the people of this region. The mark these three people from Southwest Virginia made in history will live on as long as these hills.

MOLLY TYNES:
THE FEMALE PAUL REVERE OF THE CONFEDERACY

Most Americans have heard the tale of Paul Revere and his "Midnight Ride" to warn the American colonial militia that "The British are coming! The British are coming!" as made famous in a poem by Henry Wadsworth

Longfellow. Far fewer have heard the legend of the "Female Paul Revere of the Confederacy" Molly Tynes, but it is a story worth telling. The reason her story isn't well known could be the fact there is no captivating poetry associated with her feat, or perhaps, it could be a "winners make the rules" situation where her exploits are glossed over due to the Confederacy ultimately losing the Civil War.

Molly Tynes. *West Virginia & Regional History Center.*

The story of Mary Elizabeth "Molly" Tynes begins with the outbreak of the Civil War, an event unparalleled in the history of the United States. Molly was attending Hollins Institute (now Hollins University) at the outset of the Civil War. While at Hollins, Molly Tynes studied arithmetic, English grammar, geography and history. Little did she know that she would become a part of history during the biggest event in the annals of the United States. Tynes withdrew from her educational pursuits to return to her home in Tazewell, Virginia, to care for her parents. Molly's mother was an invalid at the war's inception, which was another factor in Molly returning home from school.

The slender Molly came from a distinguished family and was described as lovely, with long, flowing golden hair that added to her appeal. Molly's father, Samuel Tynes, was a successful manufacturing businessman in the area. Samuel owned a woolen mill, a gristmill and a sawmill, all located in the Rocky Dell community of Tazewell before the Civil War. Despite being in his fifties, Samuel Tynes tried to volunteer to serve in the Confederate army, but was rejected because of his age and poor health.

Molly's brother, Achilles J. "AJ" Tynes, had gone off to war to serve in the Confederate army, where he earned the rank of captain. This gave the deeply family-oriented Molly a vested interest in the war and drew her unwavering allegiance to the Confederacy.

As the war dragged into 1863, Union troops targeted several vital Confederate holdings in Southwest Virginia, including the saltworks of Saltville, the lead mines of Austinville and the railroad at Wytheville. Colonel John T. Toland led the Thirty-Fourth Ohio Infantry, consisting of approximately one thousand soldiers, from Huntington, West Virginia, on a mission to destroy the railroad that served the area in the hopes of disrupting the transport of the lead, salt and saltpeter, in what would be a blow to the Southern cause. Colonel Toland and the Union troops encamped at the Peery Plantation, located close to the Tynes farm, at what is now known as the Ben Bolt section of Tazewell.

This is where the story gets hazy and difficult to separate fact from fiction. So many versions of the story of the Molly Tynes ride exist, and they all seem to have their own twists. Since the event occurred in the days before video could capture proof of how things transpired, it is left to historians to navigate their way through various oral and written histories to capture the essence of the truth.

A common romanticized version goes that Samuel Tynes heard of the Union plans on July 17, 1863, but wasn't physically able to spread the news himself, so, unbeknownst to her father and mother, Molly gallantly slipped out of the house at dusk and headed toward Wytheville to alert the Rebels of the upcoming attack. Molly saddled up and mounted her horse, Fashion, then made off across the mountain, alerting neighbors along the way through Burke's Garden on her path to Wytheville. It has been said she waved her bonnet while shouting, "The Yankees are coming, tell everyone the Yankees are coming!" as she sped across the mountainside on what would be a forty-plus-mile ride. This version is slightly contradicted by Molly Tynes's niece, Liza Tynes, who wrote that her grandfather (Molly's father, Samuel) helped Molly prepare for the ride and allowed her to go, well aware of the dangers, due to a strong sense of duty to their beloved Southland.

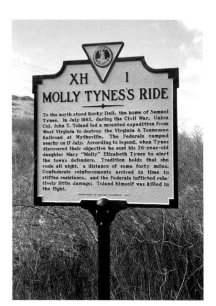

Molly Tynes's Ride historical marker.
Shane Simmons.

The legend goes that she sounded a warning at every house she encountered along the way across the four mountains on her path headed into Wytheville. It was a perilous journey where danger lurked at every turn, from wild animals to rough terrain, as the undaunted young Molly persisted. She finally arrived in Wytheville, where she alerted the townsfolk of the approaching Union attack. The news sent many in the town into a panic, with a sizable portion of the town fleeing the area while others, led by farmer Joseph Kent, were determined to stand their ground to resist the Union attack. The townspeople were described as consisting of a band of "old men and young boys" that numbered approximately 120 and met at the courthouse. Major Thomas Bowyer led a small band of Rebel troops (approximately 130 strong) to join them and prepare for the inevitable attack by the Union.

On July 18, in what is now referred to as Toland's Raid, the Union troops approached Wytheville. The local citizens, led by Joseph Kent, took the unusual (for the time) strategy of posting inside buildings and homes to fire on the attacking troops, who were mounted on horses. This technique proved to be effective, as the Yankees absorbed massive losses despite outnumbering their Rebel foes by almost three to one. The confusion brought about by the unconventional defense of Wytheville led to one of the Union commanders, Colonel William Powell, being shot by friendly fire and then captured and taken hostage by the Rebels. The other commanding officer, Colonel John Toland, attempted to rally the troops while remaining mounted on his horse. He boastfully exclaimed, "The bullet that can kill me has not been made!" But quite to the contrary, he was killed immediately after making the proclamation, struck dead by a bullet to the heart. Combined with Powell's near-fatal wound, Toland's death meant the Union forces lost both of their colonels in the first ten minutes of battle.

Eventually, the Union's massive advantage in troops began to turn the tide. The Confederate troops retreated to approximately one mile out of town, leaving behind the local citizens to fight off the attacking forces. Realizing they were greatly outnumbered, many of the local citizens dropped their weapons and fled. Due in large part to their lack of leadership, the Yankee troops were unable to take strong advantage of the situation. Before leaving town, however, the Union soldiers burned down many of the buildings and homes where the local citizens had been posted.

In the aftermath, the Union claimed victory, as they briefly captured the town, but the major outcome of the battle was that the Confederate troops and local citizens had successfully thwarted the ultimate Union goals of destroying the railroad in Wytheville, taking the lead mines in Austinville and capturing the saltworks in Saltville.

The name Molly Tynes soon grew in legend as word of her selflessness and heroics spread through the area of Southwest Virginia. One girl, who was slight in stature, took actions that proved to be larger than life.

Preacher Robert Sheffey:
The Radical Mountain Evangelist

Preacher Robert Sheffey.
Wikimedia Commons. Willard Sanders Barberry, Story of the Life of Robert Sayers Sheffey.

Southwest Virginia has seen its fair share of preachers over the decades, but only one could be seen as contributing to both legend and folklore. That man is Robert Sheffey. Preacher Sheffey, as he was often called, was larger than life. He was known for his eccentricities and his powerful prayers. Many say stories about him are frequently exaggerated or that instances happened by coincidence. Others may argue there is no limit to prayers and miracles. The world may never see eye to eye on these stories, but the stories live on either way.

Robert Sayers Sheffey was born on July 4, 1820, in Ivanhoe, Virginia. When Sheffey was two years old, his mother died, and he was taken in by his aunt in Abingdon. This family was prominent in the area and of strict Presbyterian faith. That's why when Robert Sheffey's heart was captured by the Spirit of God in a Methodist revival held in a store in Abingdon, his family was not too pleased. Sheffey studied for two years at Emory and Henry College and worked in a store, as a farmer and as a teacher to provide for his wife, Elizabeth, and six children. Eventually, his calling to become a Methodist preacher outweighed everything else.

Sheffey and his aunt argued about his decision to pursue his Methodist faith, so he departed from Abingdon. Later, Sheffey received word that his aunt was on her deathbed and he returned to Abingdon, only to find she had already passed. She had ordered a lambskin rug be given to her nephew as a sign of love and acceptance of his faith. He was known for carrying this lambskin with him everywhere, often using it to kneel on in prayer. It now is proudly on display in a Methodist church in Bluefield, Virginia.

After eleven years of marriage, Preacher Sheffey became a widower. It was then, in 1854, that he became more devoted to his circuit riding ministry and attracted more attention for his eccentricities. As a circuit-riding preacher, Sheffey rode on horseback throughout Southwest Virginia, southern West Virginia, Kentucky, North Carolina and Tennessee, spreading the gospel.

Birthplace of Robert Sheffey, moved from Ivanhoe to Giles County. *Melody Blackwell-West.*

Marker on Robert Sheffey's birthplace cabin. *Melody Blackwell-West.*

He had a deep love for all God's creatures that surpassed the understanding of most. It's said Preacher Sheffey would often dismount his horse to flip a turtle or a beetle that had ended up on its back. He even excused himself from funeral processions to remove insects from the path of wagon wheels. He had a special bond with his horse and would get down to walk to prevent the horse from carrying him up a steep hill. Tadpoles in dry holes need not worry with Preacher Sheffey around to carry water to them.

This love didn't stop with animals and insects. Preacher Sheffey would literally give the socks off his feet or the coat off his back to another who was without on a cold day. He even once gave up his beloved horse to replace another who collapsed carrying a heavy load. While these radical actions toward both man and beast were seen as an oddity, they also helped earn him a lot of respect from those living in the mountains he traveled.

Not everyone was as fond of him, however. Preacher Sheffey had a hatred of liquor and the wickedness he felt it brought to families. Much of the hype around the power of Preacher Sheffey's prayers came from the ones directed toward distilleries and their operators. One story says Sheffey prayed for the destruction of three stills along the creek near where he was preaching. The operator of the first died suddenly soon after. The second still was destroyed by a fire. And for the third, Sheffey had prayed a tree would fall, destroying it. Although there were no trees around, a storm came through, crashing a tree into the still and doing just that. It's said that still was reconstructed and later destroyed again by flooding.

Another legendary story recalls Preacher Sheffey going back to his birthplace of Ivanhoe. He stayed several weeks holding meetings and hoping for revival. After being rejected by the townspeople and witnessing fighting, drunkenness and prostitution, Preacher Sheffey cursed the town. He condemned the town to be sunken into the earth and consumed by the pits of hell. After that, the thriving mining town lost everything. The mines, rock quarry and railroads in town all closed. Soon after, the once-bustling stores also permanently closed their doors. In what some would say is Preacher Sheffey's curse, the town is now even plagued with sinkholes, at times consuming entire houses.

Not all of Sheffey's prayers led to destruction. He also was known for his powerful prayers of healing, rain during times of drought, well diggers to find water and the blessings of bees to make honey. One account even recalls a choir of angels singing the last night of a revival meeting where Sheffey was preaching. After the preaching, another well-known Methodist minister, Tyler Frazier, was leading the congregation in song when the

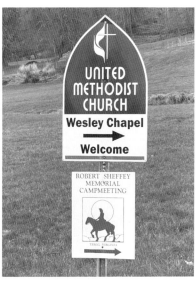

Above, left: Marker for Mountain Evangelist, Robert Sheffey, in Giles County. *Melody Blackwell-West.*

Above, right: Sign for Wesley Chapel and Robert Sheffey Memorial Camp meeting location in Giles County. *Melody Blackwell-West.*

Left: Headstone of Robert Sheffey. *Melody Blackwell-West.*

Sheffey Prayer Chapel near Wesley's Chapel in Giles County. *Melody Blackwell-West.*

crowd heard something like a swarm of bees buzzing. When the crowd rushed out of the shed to see where the noise was coming from, they heard more distinctly the low singing of the same song from above. One woman in the crowd was even convinced she heard her deceased mother's voice in the heavenly choir.

Special revivals held at Wabash Campground near Staffordsville were something Sheffey was passionate about. He advocated keeping these camp meetings going, as it pained him to see the modernization of the church being led away from such powerful gatherings. The shed used at the Wabash

Campground was destroyed by fire shortly before Sheffey's passing, and as much as he wanted to rebuild, he never was able to gather the interest or the resources to do so before his death. Now there is a Robert Sheffey Memorial Camp Meeting held annually in his honor, which starts each Friday after July 4 in Giles County.

Despite his constant travels, Sheffey did manage to remarry in 1864. Although he wasn't often at home, he had a deep love for his second wife, Eliza, who gave him a son and supported his ministry with prayer. Unfortunately, Robert Sheffey was widowed a second time in 1896. He continued his ministry as long as his health allowed. In 1902, Robert Sheffey passed away and was laid to rest in Giles County. The epitaph on his headstone reads, "Fully consecrated to God's service, he preached the Gospel without money and without price and has entered upon his reward. The poor were sorry when he died."

Since his passing, two books have been written on the life and legacy of Bob Sheffey. One of these is a biographical novel written by Jesse Carr in 1974. Later, this novel was made into a full-length movie called *Sheffey*. The passion and legends of Robert Sheffey that spread like fire throughout his lifetime in these mountains still burn on. But the eccentricity of this Appalachian John the Baptist is the gas that keeps that fire burning today.

THE INDOMITABLE MARY DRAPER INGLES

The early pioneers of Southwest Virginia faced many challenges and hardships in their lives daily from life in a rural area. One of the looming threats was being attacked by hostile Native Americans, and when those conflicts did happen, it often led to horrific violence and death. The Shawnee were one of the most common foes that roamed the area, and they could be particularly brutal.

In July 1755, an attack from an estimated sixteen Shawnee warriors occurred in a settlement known as Draper's Meadows. The residents of the settlement were caught completely off guard and offered little resistance to their attackers. At least three men, a woman and an infant were confirmed killed; a man, two women and two young boys were captured. Colonel James Patton was among the men killed. The infant was killed by the unconscionably gruesome method known as "braining" in which the young child's skull was smashed against a cabin wall. An elderly man, Philip Barger, was killed then decapitated and his head placed in a bag. The Shawnee

Statue of Mary Draper Ingles in Radford. *Shane Simmons.*

then stopped by the home of the Lybrook family and told Mrs. Lybrook to look in the bag they had brought with them, that she would "see an old acquaintance." Mrs. Lybrook was horrified when she looked in the bag and recognized the head to be that of Philip Barger.

A young mother named Mary Draper Ingles and her two sons, George and Thomas, were among the captured in what became known as the Draper's Meadow Massacre. Their captors forced them on a journey back to the Lower Shawneetown area in what is now in northern Kentucky, near the Ohio border. Mary was separated from her sons, who were adopted into families from the tribe while Mary was taken by French traders and used to sew shirts.

By October of that year, Mary and an old Dutch woman who'd been captured in Ohio hatched a plan to escape their bondage. With no supplies and no knowledge of their surroundings, the two women fled into the thick wilderness surrounding them. The two women had a plan to follow the flow of the rivers to make their way back to their old settlements. The treacherous conditions of the terrain combined with the stress and strain of scavenging for food (they were so desperate that they ate a dead snake and a decomposing raccoon at various points) soon took their toll on the women's relationship, leading to several increasingly hostile and threatening arguments between them that eventually led to their parting of ways.

Mary foraged on alone, bravely facing the continuous threat of being attacked by a wild animal, getting injured, exposure to harsh elements and any number of other threats that loomed. She crossed mountains and through forests, faced starvation and loneliness and slept out in the wild night after night in her determined quest to make it back home. After a grueling five-hundred-mile trek that took forty-two days to complete, the weak and emaciated Mary made it back to her snow-covered home in late November, where she reunited with her husband. As Mary's story spread, she was seen as a heroine for her brave trek, which represented the best of the American spirit of self-reliance and grit.

There are two primary, yet quite different, accounts of the story of Mary Draper Ingles that emerged in the aftermath. One version is by her son, John Ingles, and another is by Letitia Preston Floyd, the daughter of William and Susanna Preston. Colonel William Preston was a resident of the settlement and the nephew of Colonel Patton. Preston wasn't home at the time of the attack but recalled the events leading up to the massacre and relayed his version of what happened as was later told to him by survivors once he returned home later that evening.

As one might imagine, the version relayed by John Ingles paints Mary Draper Ingles in the most flattering light, recounting her heroics in surviving the hardships she encountered on her quest to get back home.

Historical marker in Radford describing the heroic exploits of Mary Draper Ingles. *Shane Simmons.*

Conversely, the story relayed by Letitia Preston Floyd introduces a few controversial topics into the story. According to Floyd, Mary was pregnant when she was captured and delivered a baby daughter while she was in captivity. Mary would have then abandoned the baby to make her escape, despite knowing that the customary practice of the Shawnee would have been to kill the unattended infant. Furthermore, Floyd stated that Mary Ingles and the Dutch woman had an arrangement where they cast lots to see which of the women would eat the other in the event they were on the brink of starvation. Ingles is said to have lost this contest but bribed the Dutch woman by offering her a large sum of money should she allow Mary to live. These two sensationalized details added to the drama of Mary's survival but also cast her in an unfavorable light, with many disturbed by her willingness to leave her infant child and also for being willing to consider cannibalism to survive.

The real version of all the events that transpired will never be known, but Mary Draper Ingles was unquestionably a survivor. Speaking of survivors, the band Survivor has a smash hit song "Eye of the Tiger" from the

Rocky movie soundtrack about a fighter who overcame long odds, "stayed hungry" and "went the distance." The song was about the fictional boxer Rocky Balboa but could very well have been written for Mary Draper Ingles, a real-life heroine.

FRANCIS GARY POWERS: THE COLD WAR U-2 INCIDENT

Francis Gary Powers was born in Jenkins, Kentucky, on August 17, 1929, to Oliver and Ida Powers. Francis Gary Powers grew up in Pound, Virginia, a small coal town just across the state line from Jenkins. Upon graduating from Milligan College in Elizabethton, Tennessee, Powers joined the U.S. Air Force, where he was commissioned as a second lieutenant in 1950. Powers had risen to the rank of captain by the time of his discharge in 1956.

Upon leaving the Air Force, Powers piloting talent earned him a role with the CIA's new U-2 reconnaissance program. The late 1950s began what would be dubbed the Cold War between the United States and the Soviet Union due to increasing tensions and mistrust between the two nations. The U-2 program developed from the U.S. ambitions to gather information on Soviet military activities and capabilities. The U-2 program was named for the Lockheed U-2 planes, which were capable of flying at extremely high altitudes while gathering information in various weather conditions.

Soviet intelligence knew of the flights, but before 1960 they hadn't developed a workable defense for dealing with the U-2s. On May 1, 1960, Francis Gary Powers flew out on what was thought to be a routine mission, but this time, his U-2 was clipped by a newly improved Soviet surface-to-air missile. The hit sent the U-2 falling hopelessly downward, leading to Powers ejecting from the plane before he could enact the self-destruct button. In the meantime, the Soviets accidentally struck one of their own MiG-19 planes, resulting in the death of one of their pilots.

Upon hearing of the plane being shot down, the United States quickly issued a statement claiming it had been a weather plane that had strayed off course due to the pilot experiencing oxygen problems. At the time of this statement, the CIA was unaware the plane had remained mostly intact upon crashing and that Powers had survived by parachuting. For his part, Soviet premier Nikita Khrushchev allowed the United States to think the plane had been destroyed and covered up that they had captured

Left: U-2 pilot Francis Gary Powers. *Commons: RIA Novoti.*

Below: Francis Gary Powers (*right*) and U-2 designer Kelly Johnson in 1966.

Francis Gary Powers for several days to embarrass the United States internationally. Once Khrushchev revealed the truth on May 7, the United States had already added many phony details to the story, leading to great embarrassment for President Dwight Eisenhower.

While in captivity, Francis Gary Powers was subjected to intense interrogation by the KGB over several months. Finally, Powers offered a confession and then issued an apology for his role in the espionage. On August 17, 1960, Powers was sentenced to ten years in prison, including seven years of hard labor. On February 10, 1962, Powers was released from Soviet prison as part of a prisoner exchange between the countries.

Back in the United States, Powers was greeted with mixed emotions, as many were troubled by the fact that he hadn't activated the self-destruct button and some felt that he should've taken a suicide pill to keep the Soviets from gaining intelligence. Powers faced extensive debriefing; it was finally determined that he'd conducted himself honorably and hadn't provided the Soviets with any useful intelligence.

The 1960 U-2 incident caused an increased strain on U.S.-Soviet relations that would continue for decades. For his part, Powers went to work for Lockheed as a test pilot for several years. In 1970, he wrote a book titled *Operation Overflight: A Memoir of the U-2 Incident* about his experience and, soon after, was fired by Lockheed in what many saw as retribution for unflattering revelations about the CIA. Powers would go from there to work in the radio and television industry as an airborne traffic reporter.

Francis Gary Powers's life would come to a sudden and tragic end on August 1, 1977, while covering a fire in Santa Barbara, California. On returning from covering the story, his helicopter ran out of fuel, forcing him to make an emergency landing. The story goes that Powers saw children playing in the vicinity where he intended to land, leading him to swerve to another area, which led to his demise.

Time has been much kinder to the legacy of Francis Gary Powers, as his family was given the Prisoner of War Medal, the Distinguished Flying Cross and the National Defense Service Medal in 2000 on the anniversary of the U-2 incident. On June 15, 2012, the Powers family was presented with a Silver Star for his noble service and for enduring the Soviet prison.

Francis Gary Powers is now rightfully established as an American patriot who gave a lot to our country during his lifetime for little reward.

CEDAR CREEK CHARLIE AND HIS POLKA-DOTTED HOUSE

Charlie Fields, better known as "Cedar Creek Charlie." *Susan Fields-Chandler.*

Before Silver Dollar City became Dollywood and before Carowinds was even thought up, Russell County had its own little amusement park right along beautiful Big Cedar Creek in Lebanon. Today's generation may not even realize the difficulty families of Southwest Virginia may have had traveling even two to three hours away to visit an amusement park at that time. One man, Charlie Fields, of Lebanon, wanted to make a place all families could enjoy. He made his home a welcoming and entertaining destination for families in the community, but it became something more spectacular than even Charlie could have dreamed.

Charlie was often referred to as Creek Charlie or Cedar Creek Charlie because of his home's proximity to Big Cedar Creek. His home was a humble four-room cabin built by his father around 1870 for the family of nine. The large family lived in small quarters, as was common back then, which may have been responsible for Charlie's deep family values. Charlie was born on January 30, 1887, and grew up working on the family tobacco farm. They lived off the land, raising poultry and livestock, growing their own vegetables and gathering their water from the nearby creek or well. He never attended school in order to work for the family's farm and survival.

In 1915, when Charlie was twenty-eight, his father, William, passed away. Charlie's other brothers had married and moved on, a few going into military service. It was Charlie's responsibility to carry out the work of the family farm, caring for his widowed mother, and he did so lovingly. As one could imagine, working from daylight to dark on the family farm and caring for a parent could lead to a lonely life. Charlie was a private man but found himself a girl from the Slabtown section of Lebanon to court in secret. When the girl became pregnant, Charlie was thrilled at the possibility of his own child and family, but the girl rejected his marriage proposal and shortly after married another who claimed the child as his own.

It was back to the long and lonely days for Charlie, who always remained joyous and was grateful for the company of his mother. In 1940, however,

The uniquely painted home of Cedar Creek Charlie. *Susan Fields-Chandler.*

Charlie's beloved mother, Dealie, passed away. Despite the secret of his heir around town, Charlie did have a relationship with his son. He held on to that relationship for strength, but only two years later, his only son was shipped away in the military.

Charlie had a new life to adjust to, but he wasn't going to let it get the best of him. He started painting on the outside of his house with funky patterns of squiggly lines and polka dots. He chose to paint it all in red, white and blue as a tribute to his country and his son. Neighbors at first were afraid he had gone crazy, but soon enough they were donating any leftover paint they had to help. What Charlie lacked in formal education; he made up for in creativity. After years of work, Charlie's entire house inside and out was painted from top to bottom in eccentric patterns of red, white and blue.

He didn't stop with just the house. Charlie started dreaming up attractions for the yard that children would love, such as Ferris wheels and carousels. His friends and neighbors chipped in and helped him build these model rides, which he painted all in the same patriotic colors. The larger of his two Ferris wheels was sixteen feet tall with eight seats. By the large Ferris wheel, he built five carousels with propellers at the center to have them turn. All the rides would rotate in the wind, and if the wind wasn't blowing, Charlie would spin them all himself. Kids were encouraged to touch and play with anything on Charlie's property; however, these were not operational as rides.

Crowds would flood in across the swinging bridge over the river and down the walkway Charlie had lined with tires covered in painted polka dots. Adults and kids alike wondered in amazement at the magical atmosphere Charlie had created. Parents were welcome to sit in rocking chairs and chat while the kids played on a playground up by the painted barn. Model airplanes

Home and attractions
of Cedar Creek Charlie.
Susan Fields-Chandler.

Charlie carved himself were hung from trees and filled with old dolls bought by Charlie or hand-carved puppies. Charlie welcomed the company any day of the week, but the special day for visitors was Sunday after church, when Charlie would wear his special painted outfit. From his hat down to his shoes, he had painted polka dots literally from head to toe.

The inside of his house was quite the spectacle itself. At the front door, a painted windmill spun, and a sign Charlie got a girl in town to paint to say "Welcome the doors open, come on in" hung. The floors of the living room and bedroom were painted in a bull's-eye pattern, resembling a rug. The kitchen was fully dotted, even down to his glassware and dishes.

Model airplanes hung from the painted ceiling.

But possibly the most interesting aspect of Charlie's house was his friends, the bees. Charlie created his own beehives, rarely even taking the honey of their labor, but considered them like friends. Some of these beehives were inside his home.

Charlie created chutes that ran through the wall from the exterior, providing passage for the bees. One beehive he made from an old hollowed-out television that he kept covered to block the sunlight until children come to visit. A beehive was also on each side of his fireplace. To the right, an old Victrola phonograph with the record portion converted into a beehive was fronted with glass so visitors could see the bees.

To the left was a beehive created to look like a wagon, covered in Charlie's signature polka dots and collages of pictures clipped from newspapers.

Charlie Fields was a man like no other. He left Lebanon only once in his life and vowed to never do it again. He loved his home surrounded by mountains and the family and friends that gathered there. His imagination,

Cedar Creek Charlie Sign
in Lebanon, Virginia.
Shane Simmons.

love for children and sense of humor created his magical world of entertainment and joy for everyone. Over the twenty-six years that his home was on display, it's estimated over 100,000 people visited from all over the country and even a few different countries. He never accepted a dime for admission, but often people would leave money hidden for Charlie to find later.

Thankfully, Charlie got to know and spend time with all four of his grandchildren before his death in 1966. His estate was left to his younger brother, who was unable to check in on the home as frequently as he would have liked. Unfortunately, in the 1970s, Charlie's house of art was looted. After that, his brother began selling off what was left.

Cedar Creek Charlie's artwork is still bringing smiles to faces, as some of it is displayed in various museums across the country, including the Smithsonian Museum in Washington, D.C., and the Museum of Appalachia in Clinton, Tennessee.

Charlie painted almost every dot with his finger. The hard work was a labor of love in Charlie's eyes. While he's still known today as an incredible folk artist, his only wish was one of congregation and philanthropy. Long-lasting legacies can come in all shapes—for Charlie, that shape is a polka dot.

NAPOLEON HILL:
THE MAN WHO THOUGHT AND GREW RICH

The self-help industry has been booming for a few decades now, with more and more "gurus" popping up every day looking to establish an audience of folks seeking to improve their self-esteem and create positive change in their lives. The most prominent name in the field has long been Tony Robbins, but he was far from the first practitioner of the craft. Two of the earliest self-help authors to see massive commercial success were Dale Carnegie (famous for *How to Win Friends and Influence People*) and Southwest Virginia's Napoleon Hill. Hill rose to prominence with the release of his book *Think and Grow Rich* in 1937, which has remained popular since its release, with his biographers claiming the book has sold over twenty million copies since its release. The story of how Napoleon Hill rose to prominence is a fascinating tale of how a person managed to create a dramatic change in his life, the very definition of self-help.

Napoleon Hill was born on October 26, 1883, in Pound, Virginia. His family lived in a one-room cabin, where his father supported the family by working as an unofficial and unlicensed dentist along with another common practice in the mountains, moonshining. Hill faced tragedy at a young age when his mother passed away when he was just nine years old. His first experience with writing came when he became a reporter for his father's newspaper when he was a mere thirteen years old. His life took another dramatic and unexpected turn when he was accused of impregnating a local girl. As was quite common for the time in Appalachia, this development led to a shotgun wedding between Hill and the young lady to restore her honor. Not long after the wedding, the young lady confessed that she had made up the claim, and the wedding was annulled.

Napoleon Hill reading his book *Think and Grow Rich*. From the Harvested Spiritual Mind *blog*.

After high school, Napoleon Hill went to work for the controversial former attorney general of Virginia Rufus Ayers. Ayers was a prominent early developer of the coal industry, helping to found the Virginia Coal & Iron Co., which would become the largest coal company in Virginia. One claim that has been made in association with Hill's employment for Ayers states that he received the position as a reward for helping to cover up the death of a Black bellhop, who was killed when he was accidentally shot by a drunk mine supervisor. Hill eventually left his job in the coal industry to attend law school but was forced to leave the school when he couldn't afford the tuition. He didn't let this keep him from using the title of "Attorney of Law" later in life.

Napoleon Hill married for a second time in 1903 to Edith Whitman, and they would have a child in 1905, a daughter they also named Edith. This marriage was short-lived, in part due to Napoleon Hill allegedly being physically abusive to both his wife and child. He was also said to have a weakness for frequenting prostitutes during this time, which was the final straw for the marriage. Hill moved to Mobile, Alabama, in 1907, where he helped co-found the Acree-Hill Lumber Company. This would prove to be another time of crisis in Hill's life, as the company ended up in bankruptcy in 1908 and Hill was eventually charged with mail fraud. It was during this time that Napoleon Hill claimed he encountered steel magnate Andrew Carnegie, a meeting that he would later write altered the course for the rest of his life. Many find this claim of the conversation with Carnegie to be doubtful, as no record of a meeting exists and Hill would have spent much of that time on the run from his crimes.

After leaving Alabama, Hill headed to Washington, D.C., to start all over again. He then developed what would become an early version of a multi-level marketing scheme when he started the Automobile College of Washington in 1909. The school eventually marketed itself as teaching automobile sales skills and paid students a commission for recruiting new students to take the courses. After only three years, the Automobile College of Washington closed in 1912. During this time, Hill married his third wife, Florence Elizabeth Horner, with whom he had three children.

Following the closure of his latest business venture, Napoleon Hill headed to Chicago. He accepted a position with LaSalle Extension University, and he then helped found the Betsy Ross Candy Shop. Both these ventures soon failed, as he left LaSalle shortly after starting and was soon forced out of the candy shop by the other partners in the business. It was about this time he began to claim to be an attorney. He established the George Washington Institute of Advertising, a marketing school that was built on teaching principles of success based on self-confidence. This would also prove to be short-lived, as students enrolled in the institute brought charges of fraud against Hill. He was charged with fraud by the State of Illinois for trying to raise $100,000 in capital by selling shares in his company while possessing only $1,200 in assets backing the organization.

Napoleon Hill in 1904.
www.yourprosperityfoundation.org.

Napoleon Hill would claim that he was an integral part of President Woodrow Wilson's strategy in successfully winning World War I. He went so far as to claim to be involved in negotiating the armistice with Germany. For his efforts, Hill claims to have refused to take any pay but that he was motivated by patriotism. Despite his tales of visits with President Wilson, there is no record of him ever visiting the White House, and historians doubt any of his claims took place.

Hill's next attempt at establishing a business would also run afoul of the law. He began a magazine called *Hill's Golden Rule* but was soon accused of money laundering and fraud by the Federal Trade Commission in 1919. It was claimed he misused funds that were earmarked for a veterans' charity.

In 1928, Hill moved to Philadelphia, where he was able to persuade a publishing company to release his work titled *The Law of Success.* It proved to be a major hit and propelled Hill forward in the lifestyle he'd long aspired to. He leveraged that success to make lavish purchases, including a Rolls-Royce. The Great Depression severely affected Hill, and he soon saw his six-hundred-acre property in the Catskills fall into foreclosure. He tried to resuscitate his financial position by releasing his next work in 1930, titled *The Magic Ladder to Success*, which proved to be a grand failure. This sent the now broke Hill back into his old ways of launching half-baked business ideas that would soon fold once he faced his customary charges of mismanagement and fraud.

He would continue to make outlandish claims of grandeur, once again stating he was a special advisor to a president, this time saying he assisted President Franklin D. Roosevelt with his presidency. He went so far as to say he assisted with the famed fireside chats and that he was the one who came up with the famous Roosevelt saying "The only thing we have to fear is fear itself."

In 1935, Napoleon's third wife, Florence, divorced him, leaving him with almost as many failed marriages as failed businesses. It wouldn't take long for Hill to bounce back, however, as he soon met a woman named Rosa Lee Beeland. She attended one of his lectures, and Hill was so smitten that he proposed marriage to her the following day and they were married in 1936. Still financially strapped, Hill and his new wife moved in with his son Blair in New York City. He also borrowed $300 from Blair to finish what would become his magnum opus, *Think and Grow Rich*. Rosa had a major hand in both the editing and the writing of *Think and Grow Rich*. The book outlines thirteen principles for achieving success, including desire, faith, persistence and the importance of having a definite purpose in life. Hill also emphasized the power of visualization and the importance of surrounding oneself with positive influences.

The book was a tremendous success and brought wealth back to Napoleon Hill and his new wife. They bought a home in Florida, where they became involved with a bizarre cult called the Royal Fraternity of the Master Metaphysicians. The cult was led by a man named James Bernard Schafer, who revered *Think and Grow Rich* as some sort of religious writing. It didn't take long for the marriage between Napoleon and Rosa to fall apart, and Rosa divorced Napoleon in 1940. Rosa ended up getting the vast majority of financial wealth from the book in the divorce. Adding insult to injury, Rosa would go on to marry her divorce attorney.

Looking to rebound for the umpteenth time, Napoleon Hill released a work titled *Mental Dynamite* in 1941. This proved to be another failure, and Hill continued in a downward spiral. Never one to remain on his own for too long, Hill married once again in 1943, this time a lady named Annie Lou Norman. They moved to California, where Hill hit the lecture circuit once again. He then hosted a radio show in Los Angeles for a time. He continued his tried-and-true enterprises of selling self-help courses.

In 1954, he teamed up with fellow self-help author W. Clement Stone to sell courses and launch a magazine titled *Success Unlimited*. They would successfully collaborate until the 1960s. Hill then established the Napoleon Hill Foundation in 1963, which is still in existence today.

Hill grew increasingly more open about his supposed encounters with the spirit world. His 1967 work *Grow Rich! With Peace of Mind* is filled with references to his encounters with spirits that he referred to as the Great School of Masters, who supposedly maintained a school of wisdom. He recounted in the book that he had a Master that spoke directly to him and helped with the writings of the book by revealing secrets of the world. These revelations were controversial and overshadowed the other content contained in the book.

Napoleon Hill passed away on November 8, 1970, at the age of eighty-seven. His final work, *You Can Work Your Own Miracles*, was released posthumously in 1971.

Much of Napoleon Hill's work has been questioned in the time since his passing. There are fierce debates and doubts about the many famous encounters he claimed to have had during his life. He listed some of the most famous names of the time as people he had met for interviews, a veritable who's who that includes, in part: Andrew Carnegie, Henry Ford, John D. Rockefeller, Charles Schwab, Thomas Edison, Theodore Roosevelt and many more. Thomas Edison is the only name listed of which there's any concrete proof he met. Many people believe he fabricated these stories to elevate his profile.

Some historians also question the originality of his work, claiming he took many of his ideas and teachings from other authors without giving proper credit. It has been claimed that his work was largely based on the teachings of William Walker Atkinson, an author who wrote extensively on topics related to the New Thought spiritual movement, metaphysics and the occult.

Charlatan or savior? A lot of questions linger about his story, but one thing is certain, Napoleon Hill thought, and he did grow rich.

WILLIAM CAMPBELL:
THE BLOODY TYRANT OF WASHINGTON COUNTY

The story of William Campbell is one not told nearly often enough these days, as time has almost forgotten one of our early Revolutionary War heroes. Like many men from his time, Campbell was a farmer during the days when England ruled over the thirteen original colonies. An imposing figure due to his height and muscular build, Campbell's fiery resistance to British rule led him to rise to militia leadership for the Revolutionaries. It was during this time that Campbell became one of America's first military heroes.

Born in 1745, William Campbell was one of the thirteen signers of the Fincastle Resolutions in 1775, a statement of resistance to the punitive laws known as the Intolerable Acts (which were passed by Parliament in 1774 in response to the Boston Tea Party). While the Fincastle Resolutions reaffirmed loyalty to King George III, they also served as a protest and would become a catalyst for escalating tensions between the British Crown and the colonies. These unresolved tensions continued to boil over, leading

Historical marker at the Aspenvale Cemetery concerning the heroic exploits of William Campbell. *Shane Simmons.*

to the Revolutionary War pitting numerous colonists against the British in a battle for independence.

American colonists who wished to remain under the rule of Great Britain were known as Loyalists, and those opposed were called Patriots. William Campbell was decidedly in the Patriot camp and quickly became a militia leader in that movement. Campbell had little patience or sympathy for Loyalists and is believed to have had several Loyalists executed by hanging. His intolerance of Loyalists led him to be nicknamed the "Bloody Tyrant of Washington County."

By 1780, he had risen to the title of colonel and led a militia of approximately four hundred men from Southwest Virginia. He gathered his militia in Abingdon (at what is now known as the Abingdon Muster Grounds) before leading them to a meeting at Sycamore Shoals (in present-day Elizabethton, Tennessee) to strategize with other Patriot militia leaders. The leaders decided to combine forces and pursue the Loyalists by heading south. Campbell was chosen as the overall leader of the Patriot forces by his peers as they prepared for their inevitable battle.

On September 26, 1780, Campbell and his men began the trek that would lead to combat in what is known as the Battle of Kings Mountain. The battle

Entrance to the Aspenvale Cemetery where William Campbell is buried. *Shane Simmons.*

took place on October 7 just south of Kings Mountain, South Carolina. A Loyalist militia numbering 1,105 strong led by British major Patrick Ferguson clashed against the army of Patriots with their estimated 900 soldiers.

Ferguson and the Loyalist militia had entrenched atop Kings Mountain in preparation for defending their position. The Patriot militia surrounded Kings Mountain and flanked the Loyalists by forming a *U* shape before advancing up the heavily wooded terrain. The Patriots were repelled during the initial skirmish but rallied to advance again. William Campbell rallied his men by demanding they "shout like hell and fight like devils!"

Despite superior numbers, the Loyalists were overwhelmed by the Patriots and suffered heavy casualties. Major Ferguson was among the casualties after he was shot off his horse and then dragged, alive, but with his foot caught in the stirrup across the battle line into Patriot territory. Ferguson resisted calls for his surrender and then was filled with eight musket holes after firing his pistol at his would-be captors. The Loyalist militia surrendered soon after Ferguson's demise to give the Patriot army a surprising victory.

The final tally revealed 28 dead and 62 wounded for the Patriot militia compared with 290 dead and 163 wounded for the Loyalists. There were also 668 Loyalists captured in the victory, which served as a great morale

HERE LIE THE REMAINS OF
BRIGADIER
GENERAL WILLIAM CAMPBELL

THIS STONE (1964) REPLACES THE ORIGINAL MARBLE (1823)
THE INSCRIPTION IS A TRUE COPY

The grave of William Campbell. *Shane Simmons.*

boost for the Patriots. Colonel Campbell allowed 9 men who served with Major Ferguson to face trial, where they were found guilty and sentenced to death by hanging.

Campbell returned to his home in Southwest Virginia after this battle but would soon be summoned into military action once again. Campbell and a small band of sixty soldiers joined up with Nathanael Greene's army to battle against British lieutenant General Charles Cornwallis in a skirmish at Weitzel's Mill and, shortly after, at the Battle of Guilford Courthouse. He served alongside "Light-Horse Harry" Lee (the father of Robert E. Lee) during the Battle of Guilford Courthouse, which, despite being technically deemed a loss for the Patriots, hastened the surrender of General Cornwallis at Yorktown.

Following the Battle of Guilford Courthouse, Campbell once again returned home and served in the Virginia House of Delegates for a time. On June 12, 1781, the House received a letter from the Marquis de Lafayette asking for military support to help protect Virginia. Campbell's fellow delegates, aware of his reputation as a great military leader, elected Campbell to be a brigadier general and commissioned him to assist Lafayette.

Unfortunately, Campbell's service in the capacity of brigadier general wouldn't last long. He took command of Lafayette's rifle corps early on during the Yorktown Campaign (which eventually resulted in Cornwallis's surrender). Campbell experienced chest pains and took a fever shortly thereafter before dying near Richmond on August 22, 1781, at the young age of thirty-six. Campbell was initially buried near the site of his death but was later moved back to his home in Southwest Virginia in the Seven Mile Ford area of Smyth County. His grave now rests inside the Aspenvale Cemetery, along with other members of the Campbell and Preston families.

Campbell was married to a sister of Patrick Henry, Elizabeth Henry Campbell Russell. (She went on to marry General William Russell following William's death.) Elizabeth, commonly known as "Madam Russell" is also buried at the Aspenvale Cemetery. Campbell County, Virginia, is named in General William Campbell's honor, as are the William Campbell Middle School and High School in Naruna, Virginia. General William Campbell isn't as celebrated or well-remembered as some of our other forefathers, but he left a lasting legacy of leadership and patriotism that should never be forgotten.

SMILEY RATLIFF: NO MAN IS AN ISLAND...BUT HE CAN TRY TO BUY ONE

Long before there was a Donald Trump, Appalachia had its own politically incorrect wealthy businessman with a tendency to say whatever he felt with no apologies. The man I am talking about has so many stories and legends attached to him that he would rival Davy Crockett in tall tales, a man named Arthur "Smiley" Ratliff from Buchanan County.

Arthur M. Ratliff Jr. was born on June 18, 1924, to Arthur M. Ratliff Sr. and Ida Woosley Ratliff in Buchanan County. Smiley would go on to be a star athlete in high school, leading the football team to much success as a hometown hero. After school, Ratliff fought for his country during World War II and the Korean War. His noble service earned him nineteen medals for valor, including two Purple Hearts, a Victory Service Medal and a Bronze Star for his heroics. Reminiscent of Sergeant Alvin York, Smiley earned the Bronze Star for capturing an enemy machine gun nest in 1950.

His war service to our country would have been more than enough to make him an enduring local legend; however, Smiley Ratliff was far from finished with his accomplishments. Following his military service, Ratliff

Left: Smiley Ratliff outside his Anchor Inn in Grundy. *From the* Roanoke Times, *October 16, 1988.*

Right: Smiley Ratliff. *From the* Johnson City Press, *April 25, 1982.*

became a teacher and head football coach at Hurley High School in 1952. He would lead the Rebels football team to a 28-3 record during his three-year stint as head coach.

Ratliff moved on from the teaching and coaching professions in 1954 but took his "winning principles" with him ("It doesn't matter if you win or lose, as long as you win") to the coal mining business in 1955. He had no prior knowledge or experience with mining yet still managed to build his holdings into an empire, growing it to ninety-one mines with over two thousand employees during the 1970s. He then proceeded to amass an empire of real estate holdings along with investments in cattle and local bank stock. He would go on to be the largest individual landowner east of the Mississippi River for a time.

Of all the land he owned, Smiley most frequently hung out at the Anchor Inn in Grundy. The Anchor Inn was not comparable to the Ritz-Carlton in furnishings or accommodations, which led Ratliff to famously quip, "I run it to make money, not for your comfort." Ratliff's middle initial was "M," which could have been for "Midas" in his golden ability to make money. His coal mine holdings gushed money, and Ratliff happily took in his profits.

He became increasingly frustrated with the mining business during the 1970s due to the tightening regulatory environment and his disdain for organized labor, as he operated only non-union mines. He displayed little regard for safety and was often cited and/or fined for violations by coal mine inspectors. He eventually sold out his mining business and turned to raising cattle. He built a mansion in Tazewell County that was equipped with gun towers to ward off would-be thieves.

He is said to have owned between five and fifteen Rolls-Royce cars at one time, and a commonly told story is that he would routinely spit chewing tobacco on the floor of the cars. He was seldom seen without a big "chaw" of tobacco in his jaw and, usually, with some dried-up tobacco spit in the corners of his mouth. Famously foul-mouthed, Ratliff would just as soon cuss you out as look at you (as the old saying goes). He detested the government. He was also well aware of his local celebrity and once said, "God created me to win."

The most famous story of Smiley Ratliff was his multiple attempts for several years to buy his own "nation." He heavily negotiated to buy a deserted island in the South Pacific Ocean, known as Henderson Island. He planned to build a mansion with an airstrip in his "country." A tentative agreement was reached in April 1981, but the plan fell through when the British stepped in and nixed it for environmental reasons.

Ratliff was plagued with health problems from an early age, as he suffered from a back injury that occurred during his military service. He suffered a heart attack in his mid-forties and suffered from unregulated diabetes. He didn't let any of these afflictions slow him down and lived to the ripe old age of eighty-three. He had little patience for weakness in others and expressed disbelief in the existence of the notorious "black lung" disease that has plagued so many coal miners.

An avid student of history, Smiley authored four books in his lifetime. He wrote one book titled *Stories from the Life of "Smiley" Ratliff*, which is supposedly autobiographical. As he was a master promoter and, more specifically, self-promoter, the book includes some fabulous, hard-to-believe tales that lead many to believe they were greatly embellished. Regardless, the life and times of Smiley Ratliff will not soon be forgotten, nor will the many stories cease to be told. He was a one-of-a-kind local figure and would doubtless have given "The Donald" a run for his money—both literally and figuratively.

BROTHER CLAUDE ELY:
NO GRAVE WAS GONNA HOLD HIS BODY DOWN

There ain't no grave gonna hold my body down
There ain't no grave gonna hold my body down
When I hear that trumpet sound, I'm gonna get up out of the ground
'Cause there ain't no grave gonna hold my body down

You might not be familiar with the name "Brother" Claude Ely, but if a "Mount Rushmore of Pentecostal Holiness Gospel Singers" existed, then his face would most certainly be prominently displayed. The snake-handling variety of Pentecostals seems to soak up almost all the spotlight when it comes to religion in Appalachia because, well, they pick up deadly snakes, drink poison and play with fire for crying out loud.

Having said that, the Pentecostals who don't practice snake handling make up a far greater number of churchgoers throughout Appalachia.

The life story of Brother Claude Ely doesn't need snakes, poison or fire to be entertaining. Claude Ely was born in Lee County, Virginia, in what we Appalachians call a "holler" known as Puckett's Creek near Pennington Gap on July 22, 1922. At the young age of twelve, Ely fell ill and was given what was thought to be a fatal diagnosis of tuberculosis.

Despite his grim prospects, young Claude spent much of his sick time learning to play the guitar that an uncle had given him. One day during this period in his life, Ely's family gathered around his bed to pray for him when Claude boldly proclaimed, "I'm not going to die." Claude then began to sing a song he'd written while on what doctors presumed would be his deathbed, "There ain't no grave gonna hold my body down! There ain't no grave gonna hold my body down!"

Defying the terminal medical prognosis, Claude recovered from his affliction with renewed faith and a powerful message. Claude Ely would later go on to work in the coal mines of Harlan County before and after serving in the military during World War II.

Claude felt the calling to preach in 1949, and he answered the call with a fervor as he soon earned the title of the "Gospel Ranger." Ely conducted revivals throughout eastern Kentucky, East Tennessee and Southwest Virginia, gaining a following due to his reputation for fiery sermons and impassioned singing.

Claude Ely had a larger-than-life persona, as he was an imposing, husky man who sported a gold tooth while often wearing a white cowboy hat and

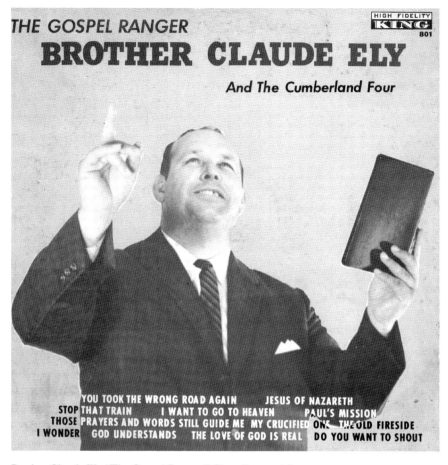

THE GOSPEL RANGER

HIGH FIDELITY
KING
801

BROTHER CLAUDE ELY

And The Cumberland Four

YOU TOOK THE WRONG ROAD AGAIN   JESUS OF NAZARETH
STOP THAT TRAIN   I WANT TO GO TO HEAVEN   PAUL'S MISSION
THOSE PRAYERS AND WORDS STILL GUIDE ME MY CRUCIFIED ONE THE OLD FIRESIDE
I WONDER   GOD UNDERSTANDS   THE LOVE OF GOD IS REAL   DO YOU WANT TO SHOUT

Brother Claude Ely "The Gospel Ranger." *Shane Simmons/album cover.*

matching white suit. As he came to each new town, Ely would drive through with a bullhorn, shouting out an invitation to his tent meetings, where he proclaimed attendees could "experience the fire and Holy Ghost."

Claude Ely was approached by King Records while ministering at the Free Pentecostal Church of God in Cumberland, Kentucky, to record his singing for commercial distribution. Ely allowed recordings to be made of one of his live sermons in 1953, making him the first Pentecostal Holiness recording artist to sign with a major record label.

Claude Ely's popularity spread even further with the release of the song he'd written as a sickly twelve-year-old boy. "There Ain't No Grave (Gonna Hold My Body Down)" went on to become an anthem and a staple of Pentecostal churches for years to come. Claude Ely would spend the remainder of his

Brother Claude Ely. *King Records promotional photo.*

life preaching fire and brimstone while singing with that same conviction to save lost souls.

Among Ely's fans was one Gladys Presley, mother of a young man you might know as Elvis Presley. Gladys is said to have brought Elvis to at least one of Ely's tent revivals to have the preacher lay hands on them in prayer. Elvis was later inspired by Ely's version of "There's a Leak in This Old Building/You've Gotta Move" to sing a rendition of the song under the name "We're Gonna Move" for his film *Love Me Tender*.

On May 7, 1978, Ely suffered a massive heart attack in front of the congregation at his home church of Charity Tabernacle in Newport, Kentucky (just across the river from Cincinnati, Ohio). Ely was playing the organ and singing "Where Could I Go but to the Lord" when he suddenly fell backward midway through the song. Churchgoers began to cry out and pray over him to no avail; Claude Ely passed away at the age of fifty-five.

Ely was brought back to Southwest Virginia, where he is buried at a cemetery in the town of Dryden in Lee County.

Johnny Cash recorded an acclaimed version of Ely's "Ain't No Grave" that was released posthumously in 2010. (The song also included musical contributions by the Avett Brothers.)

Although he has been gone for over forty years, Claude Ely is still well remembered and beloved in many Pentecostal corners of Appalachia. Few songs can whip a Pentecostal crowd into a sing-along/clap-along frenzy like a passionate rendition of "Ain't No Grave" in a little country church deep in these hills—can I get an amen?

II

LEGENDARY EVENTS OF SOUTHWEST VIRGINIA

THE SHOCKING HILLSVILLE MASSACRE

The most excitement usually seen in the sleepy little town of Hillsville is the annual flea market that takes over the entire town for a weekend. The last thing you'd ever expect would be a deadly courthouse shootout, but that is exactly what took place on March 14, 1912. The fact that five people died in the aftermath of the gunfire is undisputed, but just who fired the first shot is not nearly so clear and has been a matter of debate for well over a century. The event is commonly known in the area as the Hillsville Massacre and still haunts the history of Carroll County.

The story begins innocently enough in the early spring of 1911, when the town held a corn-shucking bee on a Saturday evening. The bee included contests for fun and amusement and one seemingly harmless tradition where if a young man found a rare colored "red ear" of corn, then he would be allowed to kiss the girl of his choosing. A red ear was discovered by a young man named Wesley Edwards, who ended up kissing a girl that was already "spoken for" by a boy named Will Thomas, which led to a skirmish between the two young men. Unwilling to drop it, the following morning Will Thomas went to the church Edwards was attending and called him out to fight. According to the version later told by Edwards, Will Thomas and three other young men began to assault him, which led to his cousin Sidna Edwards joining in the fracas. In the fallout, Wesley and Sidna Edwards faced several charges, including assault with a deadly weapon and disorderly

The Carroll County Courthouse in 1912. *Library of Congress.*

conduct. The brothers evaded arrest and slipped into Mt. Airy, North Carolina. Getting wind of their whereabouts, the local authorities issued a warrant for their arrest and notified the sheriff of Surry County, North Carolina, and they were soon apprehended and prepared for extradition.

Carroll County deputy Thomas Samuels and a driver, Peter Easter, headed to pick up the Edwards brothers from North Carolina authorities at the state line. The buggy carrying the handcuffed Edwards brothers passed by property owned by their uncle Floyd Allen. Floyd Allen was a prominent local businessman who, in addition to his generosity, was known for having an explosive temper. The sight of his nephews being paraded past his family property set off the hotheaded Allen, who confronted Samuels and Easter. Floyd Allen blocked the path of the buggy with his horse, which prompted Deputy Samuels to pull his pistol on him in an attempt to stop Allen. Allen called his bluff and a fight ensued, during which Floyd Allen took away Deputy Samuels's gun and proceeded to pistol-whip Samuels. Peter Easter elected to flee the melee and headed back to Hillsville but, in the process, fired a shot in the direction of Floyd

Allen and wounded him in the finger. Having beaten Samuels unconscious and left for dead, Floyd Allen freed Wesley and Sidna Edwards from their handcuffs and left the scene. Saying his only intention was to have the boys freed of the shame of wearing handcuffs, Floyd Allen later brought the brothers to turn themselves in. Wesley and Sidna Edwards were quickly tried, convicted and sentenced. Despite their sentencing, neither of the brothers served time in jail but, rather, on work release.

The Republican commonwealth's attorney, William Foster, was a fierce opponent of the Allen family, having defeated Walter Allen in a hotly contested election the prior cycle. Floyd Allen and the rest of the Allen clan were already furious with Foster for not bringing any charges against the other boys involved with the fight at the church. At the behest of Foster, a grand jury investigated the incident that led to the escape of the Edwards brothers. The grand jury indicted Floyd Allen for assault and battery and set a trial. Before the trial, it was rumored that Floyd Allen threatened to kill Thomas Samuels if he testified against him in the case. Samuels immediately fled town on hearing the news, believing the threats to be quite credible. Floyd Allen denied ever making the threat.

The trial of Floyd Allen began on March 13, 1912. Since Thomas Samuels had skipped town, the only witness to the incident was Peter Easter. After the trial, the jury couldn't come to a quick verdict, meaning they would

The Carroll County Courtroom in 1912. *Library of Congress.*

be sequestered in a local hotel overnight before reconvening. Fear and tension began to build at the prospect of a guilty verdict, with many local officials arming themselves in case of a conflict. Judge Thornton Massie and Sheriff Lewis Webb braced for expected trouble. The next day, the jury met again and a verdict was finally reached. The courtroom was full, and several members of the Allen family were in attendance—many of them were strapped, adding to the palpable tension. The verdict was read, and Allen was declared to be guilty. According to legend, Allen is said to have told the judge, "If you sentence me on that verdict, I will kill you!" Judge Massie then sentenced Floyd Allen to a term of one year in prison. Allen's defense attorney, David Winton Bolen, later recounted that

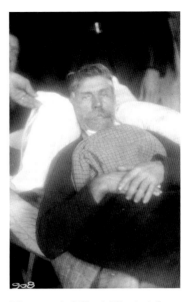

The wounded Floyd Allen in jail. *Library of Congress.*

Floyd Allen said words to the effect, "I just tell you, I ain't a-goin.'" Almost immediately, shots rang out in the courtroom.

No one can say for certain who took the first shot, with some saying Floyd Allen drew his weapon first. Floyd Allen claimed that Sheriff Webb took the first shot and missed and that Deputy Clerk Dexter Goad took the second shot and hit Floyd Allen with the bullet. This shot caused Floyd Allen to fall to the ground. According to Floyd Allen, it was only then that he returned fire. A hail of gunfire filled the courtroom, and the Allen clan made their escape, firing away for cover as they fled. In the wake of the shooting, four men lay dead: Judge Massie, Commonwealth's Attorney Foster, Sheriff Webb and jury foreman Augustus Fowler. A nineteen-year-old female witness against Allen, Elizabeth Ayers, died the next day from wounds she suffered from being shot in the back while fleeing the courtroom. Seven others were wounded, Floyd Allen and Dexter Goad among them. It has been said that fifty-seven bullets were found in the courtroom in the aftermath, the gun battle having lasted an estimated ninety seconds.

Floyd Allen had suffered several wounds and was too weak to leave town, so he holed up in the Elliott Hotel. Upon discovering his whereabouts, officers were sent to arrest him. Floyd attempted suicide before they could arrest him by cutting his own throat with a pocketknife, but he was soon subdued and taken into custody. An odd law was in effect in those days that said once a sheriff died, his deputies had no legal authority to arrest, so this posed a huge problem in the Allen case. Virginia governor William Hodges Mann enlisted the infamous Baldwin-Felts Detective Agency (best known for their role in enforcing the "law" for coal mining companies against miners) to track down and arrest suspects in the courthouse shooting. Rewards were posted for five suspects in the shooting: Claud Allen, Freel Allen, Sidna Allen, Sidna Edwards and Wesley Edwards. Three of the five were captured within a month, but the final two, Sidna Allen and Wesley Edwards, managed to escape and make it out to Des Moines, Iowa, before being captured after several months. Their location had been given up by an informant.

Floyd Allen was the first member of the Allen clan brought to trial for the murders in the courthouse, charged with the first-degree murder of Commonwealth Attorney William Foster. The prosecution intended to paint the picture of a grand conspiracy by the Allen clan to murder the judge, prosecutor, law enforcement, members of the jury, etc. Essentially, the Allens would kill anyone involved in the conviction of Floyd Allen, according to the prosecutor's case. Furthermore, the prosecution claimed that the gun battle began due to shots being fired by Floyd Allen and Claud Allen. David Winton Bolen, who'd served as a defense attorney for Floyd Allen in the original trial, was now a star witness for the prosecution. Bolen testified that Claud Allen fired the first shot at Judge Massie, followed by another shot by Sidna Allen at the judge, leaving him dead. Likewise, the other defense attorney for Allen in the original trial, Walter Tipton, testified that he witnessed Floyd Allen firing his pistol. Two other witnesses, then

The Allen Clan. *Mt. Airy Museum of Regional History.*

sheriff George Edwards and Sidney Towe, both testified they heard Floyd Allen proclaim he would put a "big hole in the courthouse" if the trial didn't go his way before the shooting.

In his defense, Floyd Allen claimed that Deputy Clerk Dexter Goad had fired the first shot, stating that both he and the commonwealth attorney both had contempt for the Allen family due to political differences. Furthermore, they stated it was Goad who had shot Elizabeth Ayers in the crossfire, a charge Goad vehemently denied. Allen did admit to shooting at H.C. Quisinberry (an unsubstantiated legend has it that Quisinberry confessed to firing the first shot in the courthouse many years after the shootout) and at two other people, whom he couldn't identify. Deputy Clerk Goad confessed that he fired the second shot that struck Floyd Allen. Numerous other witnesses were called, and several versions of the events were described, but most all of them seemed to damn Floyd Allen in the case. On May 18, 1912, the jury came back with a guilty verdict that sentenced Floyd Allen to death in the electric chair.

In July 1912, a separate trial was held for Floyd's son Claud, and another guilty verdict was handed down for the first-degree murder of Commonwealth Attorney Foster and second-degree murder in the death of Judge Massie. Claud was also sentenced to death in the electric chair. Several other members of the Allen clan pleaded guilty to their roles in the massacre. Sidna Allen pleaded guilty to second-degree murder in the death of Judge Massie and voluntary manslaughter in the death of Commonwealth Attorney Foster, for which he received a thirty-five-year prison sentence. Wesley Edwards was sentenced to twenty-seven years in prison; Sidna Edwards was sentenced to fifteen years; and Freel Allen was sentenced to eighteen years. Victor Allen and Barnett Allen were acquitted.

Liens were placed on the property and possessions of the wealthy Floyd Allen and Sidna Allen, and an auction was held where proceeds from the sale of the property would go to the surviving members of the victims of the murders.

Floyd and Claud Allen would not go quietly following their convictions. A plan was hatched to have Lieutenant Governor James Taylor Ellyson commute their sentences while he was presiding over the Commonwealth of Virginia in the absence of Governor Mann, who was out of state in Pennsylvania. Mann got word of the plan and quickly returned to Virginia to put a stop to the transaction. After a brief power struggle, the death sentence was upheld, and the executions went on as originally planned. On March 28, 1913, at 11:20 p.m., Floyd Allen was electrocuted, with Claud's execution being conducted a mere eleven minutes later. Floyd Allen's original tombstone read that he was "judicially murdered."

Sadly, the killing didn't end there. Floyd's brother, Jack Allen, would get into a dispute with a moonshiner, Will McGraw, in Mt. Airy, North Carolina, over the case on March 17, 1916. During the brawl, McGraw drew his pistol and shot Allen twice, and Allen died at the scene.

In 1922, Governor Elbert Lee Trinkle pardoned Freel Allen and Sidna Edwards. In 1926, Governor Harry Flood Byrd pardoned Sidna Allen and Wesley Edwards.

The Hillsville Massacre made national headlines and drew much unwanted attention to the town of Hillsville before being knocked out of the public's consciousness by the sinking of the *Titanic*. The nation moved on from the story, but the Hillsville Massacre still lingers in the hills and hollers of Carroll County. The townsfolk of Hillsville know that, unlike the famous song from the Humphrey Bogart movie *Casablanca* would have you believe, the more correct line would be, "You must remember this, a kiss is not just a kiss sometimes."

THE LAST RIDE OF LUKE THE DRIFTER

The Burger Bar is located at an intersection of State Street in Bristol, Virginia, just a shade over the Tennessee line. The restaurant first opened in 1942 and, according to local legend, has long been said to have been the last place anyone saw the great country singer Hank Williams Sr. alive. The facts have been debated and disputed for years, but that is the story told by the last person to see him before his demise, his driver that night, Charles Carr.

On New Year's Eve 1952, Hank Williams was taken by wheelchair and loaded into his baby-blue Cadillac convertible, headed out of the Andrew Johnson Hotel in Knoxville, Tennessee, for a show in Canton, Ohio. Williams, said to be loaded up on a host of various medicines, was put in the back seat of his car and wrapped up in a blanket to sleep for the majority of the ride as Charles Carr, a teenager, was assigned to drive the honky-tonk legend to the concert destination. A little before midnight, Carr dropped off in Bristol to grab a bite to eat at what is now known as Burger Bar (at that time it was called Snack King). Carr would later say that he asked Williams if he'd like something to eat from there too, to which Hank declined, simply saying, "No." It would be the last word Hank would utter and the last time anyone would see him alive.

A bit farther down the road across the state line in West Virginia, Charles Carr checked on Williams at a service station when he noticed Hank's blanket had fallen off. A frantic Carr got no response from the lifeless figure in the back seat, and a closer inspection showed that Hank Williams's body was cold and stiff, which caused Carr to go into a great panic. He raced to explain the gravity of the situation to the owner of the service station, who

Opposite: Hank Williams in 1951. *Promotional photo for WSM.*

Right: Burger Bar in Bristol, Virginia. *Shane Simmons.*

called the police, and Williams was then sped to a hospital in Oak Hill, West Virginia. Despite the best efforts of the medical professionals at the hospital, they were too late to save him, and the twenty-nine-year-old Williams was pronounced dead on New Year's Day 1953.

An autopsy showed that Hank Williams had died of heart failure attributed to a heart attack. Rumors, legends and myths have surfaced ever since claiming various other causes of death, from foul play to suicide. Many, including Hank's wife, believed there was more to the story than a simple heart attack. Supposedly, several empty beer cans and handwritten lyrics to an unfinished song were found in the back seat of the car driven that night.

One thing is certain: the man nicknamed Luke the Drifter took his last ride somewhere on a lonely road in Appalachia on that fateful night. It brings to mind some lyrics made famous by Hank Williams: "Take my advice or you'll curse the day you started rollin' down that lost highway."

Murderess or Martyr?

Few things are as intriguing as a small-town murder, especially when one is based on a true story from the normally tranquil hills of Appalachia. This complicated tale comes from the town of Pound in Wise County, Virginia.

The story of Edith Maxwell is one that made national headlines when she stood accused of murdering her father, Trigg Maxwell, on July 21, 1935. Edith, a popular twenty-one-year-old teacher, had gotten home at midnight from being out with her beau, Raymond Meade, on a date, or "courting" as it was often called in the area during this time. Trigg Maxwell was livid when she came through the door at such a late hour and flew into a blind rage, claiming that decent women were always home by nine o'clock. He informed her that he was going to whip her as punishment. Those are the accepted facts of the case, but what transpired afterward soon became the subject of much speculation and conjecture.

Trigg Maxwell rushed at Edith to commence her whipping, and soon after, a neighbor heard a loud racket coming from the house. The neighbor rushed to the Maxwell home, only to find an unconscious Trigg Maxwell lying on the kitchen floor in a pool of blood. Trigg bled out within fifteen minutes, and later that morning, Edith Maxwell and her mother, Anne, were arrested for his murder by Sheriff J.P. Adams. Anne Maxwell was released later that day on a $3,000 bond, while Edith was kept incarcerated in the Wise County jail. Being such a small town, many conflicts arose, such as the jailor being Edith's uncle Jim Dotson.

On July 23, a special grand jury indicted both Anne and Edith Maxwell for the murder of Trigg Maxwell, just a day before his funeral was held in Pound. Anne was eventually cleared of all charges. Many people at the time believed Anne was the actual killer and that Edith took the fall to cover up her mother's crime.

Rumors began to fly around town that the murder weapon was potentially either an axe, a skillet or, even, a high heel shoe. Trigg Maxwell was cast by locals as a brutish, controlling father with a penchant for drinking alcohol, which amplified his volatile personality when he was on a bender. City newspapers soon seized on the captivating story, casting Edith as a hillbilly sweetheart and presenting her as the girl-next-door victim of her father's overly strict ways. Edith was quite photogenic, and her physical attractiveness was used to garner further sympathy. The *Washington Post* even went so far as to set up a defense fund for her.

In contrast to the fawning treatment of Edith Maxwell, the national media wasn't as kind concerning the depiction of the townspeople of Pound and the surrounding area. Locals in Wise County began to resent the unflattering way in which the area was presented by these city newspapers. Reporters were perceived as trying to dredge up stories looking for preconceived hillbilly stereotypes of moonshining, violence and political

Father Slayer in Cell

MOUNTAIN GIRL FACES 25 YEARS BEHIND BARS

EDITH MAXWELL IN JAIL — (STORY ON PAGE 1)
Read Her Fascinating Life Story Beginning in Next Sunday's Examiner

An imprisoned Edith Maxwell peering out her jail cell. *From the* San Francisco Examiner, *December 13, 1935.*

corruption. The unflattering representation of Wise County in newspaper articles eventually led to an unfair backlash in some quarters against Edith Maxwell. A series of five articles written by Fulton Lewis, a writer for Universal Service, was published in the *Washington Herald*, labeling it as the "curfew murder," and went to great lengths to reinforce stereotypes of the residents as hillbillies who lived by a "mountain code" of justice. This series further alienated the local population and resulted in more hostility toward outside news media.

Edith Maxwell stood trial beginning on November 18, and it became a crowded spectacle as locals and news media jockeyed for position to witness the proceedings. The news media contrasted Edith Maxwell in a glowing manner versus the local jury, in what sounded more like coverage of a fashion show than a murder trial:

Into the jury box filed 12 men, their clothes rough and their boots caked with mud from the trail of the lonesome pine.

Edith came into the court, a jaunty brown hat on the right side of her head and a wisp of a veil tumbling to her nose. Her smart white shirtwaist, brown skirt, and suede shoes were strangely out of place in the backwoods courtroom. [Harry Ferguson, United Pres staff correspondent, as printed in the November 18, 1935 edition of the Brooklyn Times Union, page 8.]

The newspaper article went on to claim:

There is no appeal she can make against the prejudices of the mountaineers, but in the eyes of the law she can and will plead manslaughter in the process of self-defense.

During the trial, Edith Maxwell confessed to killing her father with the sharp edge of her high heel shoe but stated it was done in self-defense against her father's savage attack. The trial wrapped up on November 19 and was left in the hands of the jury. The jury, made up of twelve men and no women, handed back the verdict for Edith that was read at 7:05 p.m. in which she was convicted of the murder of Trigg Maxwell. She was sentenced to twenty-five years in the state penitentiary, which resulted in a national outcry against the guilty verdict in the media. Edith Maxwell was then thrust forward as a prominent face of women's rights.

In the aftermath of the trial, a Richmond attorney, M.J. Fulton, was employed by the National Woman's Party to assist in appealing the case. Among a laundry list of claims, Fulton stated that the fact neither the jury nor the grand jury included any women was a violation of Edith Maxwell's constitutional rights and warranted a new trial. This motion was entered on December 31. On January 8, attorney and vice chairwoman of the National Woman's Party Gail Laughlin joined her defense team and declared the verdict to be "a gross miscarriage of justice." Later in January, Judge W.A. Skeen, who'd presided over the original trial, denied the motions for a new trial.

Undeterred, the defense team continued probing for angles to force a new trial. Their efforts were rewarded by the State Supreme Court of Appeals, which granted a new trial in a ruling on September 11, 1936, when it deemed the evidence on record was not sufficient to warrant the first-degree-murder conviction. Edith was released from jail on September 19 on a $6,000 bond while awaiting a new trial. In the meantime, Judge Skeen was forced to recuse himself from the retrial when it was determined he was a distant relative of Trigg Maxwell. Governor George C. Peery named a new judge, Ezra Carter, to preside over the new trial.

The second trial began on December 9, 1936, and stretched out until December 17, when the new jury convicted Edith Maxwell of second-degree murder and recommended a sentence of twenty years. Judge Carter imposed the jury's recommended sentence, and things looked grim for Edith. She served four years of the sentence before being pardoned by Virginia governor James Price in 1941. A letter sent to the governor from First Lady Eleanor Roosevelt lobbying for the pardon was a major factor in this development. Upon her release from prison, Edith changed her name to Ann Grayson and moved away to Florida, where she began a new life. Edith Maxwell/Ann Grayson eventually passed away in Indiana in 1979 in anonymity.

The Edith Maxwell story is another case where major media jumped on a story, added their spin to it and sensationalized the details to sell papers, regardless of facts. Appalachian "hillbillies" plus murder is a formula that always seems to work for generating attention. The story of Edith Maxwell is a good reminder that the truth and justice are often meted out, not served.

Murder Is in Your DNA

Wanda Faye McCoy was a nineteen-year-old housewife with no known enemies who lived in the sleepy town of Grundy, Virginia. Her peaceful life came to a sudden and brutal end on March 10, 1981, when she was raped and then savagely stabbed by an intruder. Her unassuming life might not have been newsworthy, but her death made national headlines for years.

Police investigating the crime scene determined there had been little to no struggle, suggesting that she likely knew her murderer. Suspicion immediately fell on her brother-in-law, Roger Keith Coleman, as he had access to the home and a reputation as a high-tempered loner with a shady past. Coleman was a coal miner in Grundy who had shown up for work that night but was laid off upon arriving at the mine.

The prosecution, led by Commonwealth Attorney Michael "Mickey" McGlothlin, gathered evidence for the case against Coleman. Physical

Roger Keith Coleman on the cover of *Time* magazine. *From* Time *magazine, May 18, 1992.*

evidence included a blood sample on Coleman's clothes that matched McCoy's type and a hair found on McCoy that matched Coleman's hair. Other evidence brought against Coleman showed he had a prior conviction for an attempted rape as well as a witness in prison who testified that Coleman had confessed to the crime.

The defense countered that Coleman had a credible alibi, with multiple witnesses giving affidavits on his behalf. They also contended that DNA tests on the semen found on McCoy's body suggested more than one person. Also, despite the initial appearance of a lack of struggle, the victim had cuts on her arm and the front door had pry marks on it, suggesting maybe it had been a forced entry.

The trial ended in 1982 with Roger Keith Coleman convicted in the murder of Wanda McCoy and sentenced to death. Coleman spent the better part of the next ten years on death row. Multiple appeals were filed on behalf of Coleman during this time, with all being denied. New DNA testing was conducted in 1990, with the results further damaging Coleman's case, as it revealed that he fit into the 2 percent of the population who could have committed the crime.

For his part, Roger Keith Coleman howled that he was getting railroaded by a flawed justice system. His cries of innocence began to gain a national following as more and more people lined up seeking clemency on his behalf. Virginia governor Doug Wilder's office received more than thirteen thousand calls and letters concerning the case.

The pressure continued to mount on Governor Wilder to stay the execution as more and more national media attention began to cast doubt on the case. The *LA Times* and *New York Times* did articles on the case and Coleman's plight. *Time* magazine went so far as to put Coleman on the cover of the May 18, 1992, edition with the caption "This Man Might Be Innocent This Man Is Due To Die." Coleman was also interviewed by Phil Donahue on the *Donahue* show just days before the execution was to take place, among a flurry of other television appearances.

The day of execution arrived, and Coleman still frantically looked for any avenue to escape his fate. His last meal would be pepperoni pizza, fudge cookies and a 7 Up soft drink, which he shared with the executive director of Centurion Ministries, James McCloskey. Centurion Ministries was an organization dedicated to freeing prisoners that it deemed to be innocent, and it had adopted Coleman as a worthy cause.

Unbeknownst to the public, Governor Wilder had conceded to give Roger Keith Coleman a last-minute lie detector test—which he failed. The Supreme Court also declined to intervene, which proved to be Coleman's last hope. After a brief delay, the execution proceeded, with Coleman giving his final words from the electric chair, "An innocent man is going to be murdered tonight. When my innocence is proven, I hope Americans will recognize the injustice of the death penalty as all other civilized nations have."

At 11:38 p.m., Roger Keith Coleman was pronounced dead, but his story was far from over. Centurion Ministries, among other anti–death penalty groups, continued to use Roger Keith Coleman as the poster boy for their cause. Efforts continued in the years following Coleman's execution with the belief that advancements in DNA testing would clear his name. Finally, Governor Mark Warner gave in to the pressure and agreed to allow the DNA to be looked at again. The results came back, which conclusively proved to match Coleman with no exclusions to a nineteen-million-to-one probability. The DNA findings were a victory for the justice system and a blow against opponents of the death penalty.

The entire U.S. justice system might have been changed had the DNA results been different. Good, reasonable people disagree on the death penalty, so that debate rages on to this day. Roger Keith Coleman was a convincing liar with an amazing ability to appear the innocent victim. The shame of the media attention at the time was the attention and sympathy given to a cold-blooded murderer, with Wanda McCoy being lost as an afterthought in the story. Despite the overwhelming preponderance of the evidence, there's still a small but quite vocal contingent that believes in Coleman's innocence. It serves as proof of an old saying attributed to Abraham Lincoln, "You can fool some of the people all the time."

Big A Mountain Helicopter Crash

It was a cloudy Thursday afternoon in Buchanan County on May 27, 1982. The area had just been hit by major flash flooding the day before, resulting in $400,000 in road damage and almost $1 million worth of property damage. A helicopter owned by Jewell Smokeless Coal Company was hauling two Norfolk and Western Railroad employees to scope out rail lines in the Dismal area, which had been blocked by mudslides.

John Lytton was a division engineer for maintenance of the Pocahontas Division, and Raymond Daniels was a roadmaster.

The day was clear despite the severe weather the night before. The pilot was Robert Wood, an employee of Jewell Smokeless, who was familiar with the area. Yet somehow, the helicopter struck a power line and came surging to the ground. The pilot and both passengers were killed in the wreckage. The fact the helicopter hit a power line was apparent, but the reason why was unknown.

The accident occurred about ten miles from Grundy, leaving debris scattered throughout a large area, including Big A Mountain. Big A Mountain sits between the towns of Honaker and Council. Located just over the Russell County line, Big A Mountain is the highest peak in Buchanan County. It's known for its winding roads, spectacular views, an interesting old fire tower and the site of the wreckage of this crash.

Large pieces of metal were left on Big A Mountain near a tree said to have caught one of the crash victims. It's said a local was first to the scene when he saw the man stuck in the tree limbs, not yet crossed over and moaning in pain. He was not able to help the man and by the time rescue crews arrived, it was too late.

As time passed, the tragedy became less talked about, but some curiosity remained. Over the years, some have ventured out to the area of the ruins. They have said they feel a sudden drop in temperature and cold chills. The smell of decay fills the air around the site despite all the years that have passed.

There's also been accounts of moaning sounds coming from the tree limbs overhead. The same tree the man was said to have breathed his last breath in and left bones unable to be recovered in.

The wreckage site of the 1982 helicopter crash on Big A Mountain has since been known as one of the most haunted locations in the area. The tragic deaths of the three men came as a major shock to residents of Southwest Virginia. Perhaps the man who met his end on Big A Mountain has still not come to terms with it himself.

GOD ALONE KNOWS WHICH WAS RIGHT

A prime example of the literal meaning of the "brother against brother" phrase in the Civil War involved two Appalachian brothers who became brigadier generals for the opposing sides, James B. Terrill for the Confederacy and William R. Terrill for the Union, the sons of William H. Terrill. In all, William had four sons serve during the war, with three serving in the Confederacy—James, Robert and Thomas—with just William siding with the Union.

William Rufus Terrill was already serving in the U.S. Army when the Civil War began. Leaving no doubt as to his allegiance, William telegraphed General Winfield Scott, "I am now and ever will be true to my oath and my country. No one has any authority to tender my resignation. I will be in Washington as soon as possible." He was commissioned as a captain of the Fifth U.S. Artillery, and this decision to remain loyal to the Union resulted in his father disowning him. William participated in the Battle of Shiloh, which earned his promotion to brigadier general of the Thirty-Third Brigade of the Army of the Ohio. He led his inexperienced infantry troops into the Battle of Perryville, where they were attacked and pushed back by Confederate troops. Terrill reorganized his troops and returned them to the fight to support the Union left flank. Terrill was mortally wounded when a Confederate artillery shell exploded near him, sending shrapnel into his

Union general William R. Terrill (*left*) and Confederate general James B. Terrill. *Public domain.*

chest. At seeing the massive wound and seemingly predicting his dire fate, Terrill is said to have muttered to himself, "My poor wife, my poor wife." The twenty-eight-year-old William died from the wound later that day despite his doctor's best efforts to save him.

James Barbour Terrill was practicing law in Bath County, Virginia, when the Civil War erupted. Upon Virginia's secession from the Union, James wrote a letter to Virginia governor John Letcher saying, "I deem it my duty to make a formal tender of my services in a military capacity to the Governor of the state." Terrill then hurried to Harpers Ferry to serve in the new Confederate army, where he was appointed as a major of the Thirteenth Virginia Infantry. James participated in several major battles of the war, including both battles of Bull Run/Manassas, Antietam, Fredericksburg and Spotsylvania Courthouse.

He earned a promotion to the rank of colonel for his exemplary service. James met his death on the battlefield at the young age of twenty-six during the Battle of Totopotomoy Creek/Bethesda Church. James was gravely wounded when a Union bullet ripped through his body while he was leading his men into battle. He slowly struggled to his feet despite profusely bleeding from this wound to rally his troops for another push, only to be shot in the head and killed. He was originally buried on the battlefield by Union troops, but his father later had his body exhumed for a burial closer to home. James Terrill had previously been nominated and was posthumously confirmed as a brigadier general by the Confederate States of America's Senate.

A third brother, Lieutenant Thomas Terrill, also died during the war, perishing after being mortally wounded during the Battle of Gettysburg. The fourth brother, Lieutenant Robert Terrill, was wounded during the Battle of Gaines Mill on June 27, 1862, but managed to survive the war.

According to a story printed in *Harper's Weekly*, legend has it that their father had a monument erected in honor of his sons that read, "This monument erected by their father. God alone knows which was right." Some have questioned the validity of the claim of such a monument's existence, but the sentiment of the statement is certainly on point. No other event in our nation's history is as captivating and tragic as the Civil War, and Appalachia was at the heart of the conflict.

COAL MINERS WEREN'T THE ONLY VICTIMS OF COAL MINING

Southwest Virginia is synonymous with coal mining dating back over a century. One of the major coal-producing companies was the Jewell Ridge Coal Corporation in Jewell Ridge. Unfortunately, coal mining has a long history of labor disputes, and Jewell Ridge Coal was not immune to these issues. Jewell Ridge became engaged in a contentious court case that made it to the United States Supreme Court. The case became so heated that it led to the ugliest public exchange between justices in the history of the highest court in America.

The dispute between the United Mine Workers of America (UMWA) union and Jewell Ridge Coal Corporation arose when the two parties could not agree on when the workday began for coal miners. The UMWA contended that miners should be paid for the time it took them to travel underground from the portal entry back to the working face of the mine. In some cases, it could take fifteen to twenty minutes to travel the distance, and the union felt the miners should be able to accrue this as paid work time. Jewell Ridge Coal held that the miners weren't working during this time, so it shouldn't count as part of their work schedule, asserting that their work time shouldn't start until they began the process of extracting coal.

On May 7, 1945, the U.S. Supreme Court ruled 5–4 in favor of the UMWA, interpreting Section 7(a) of the Fair Labor Standards Act of 1938 to include underground travel as part of the workday. The result led to bitter hostilities between Justice Hugo Black, who voted in favor of the UMWA, and Justice Robert Jackson, who sided with Jewell Ridge Coal. The main point of contention was Justice Jackson's vehement opposition to Justice Black not recusing himself from the case due to a clear conflict of interest. The conflict arose from the fact that the chief counsel for the UMWA, Crampton Harris, had been Hugo Black's former law partner in Alabama. The fact that Black had been the deciding vote in the case infuriated Jackson, and he continued to stew over the outcome, despite being intensely involved as the chief American prosecutor in the famed Nuremberg Trials, where individuals associated with Nazi Germany were tried for war crimes committed during World War II. Justice Jackson was also irritated that Justice Black had rushed to have the verdict handed down without the customary opinion and dissent. Jackson surmised that Black was in such a hurry to affect the ongoing negotiations between the UMWA and the coal company, giving the union a negotiating advantage.

Meanwhile, while Jackson was in Nuremberg, the chief justice position opened up on the Supreme Court with the unexpected death of Harlan Stone on April 22, 1946. Justice Jackson had been tapped by President Franklin D. Roosevelt to become the next chief justice. The problem with that plan is that President Roosevelt died while in office, so Harry Truman was now the president, and he was under no obligation to fulfill Roosevelt's wishes. Two opposing factions developed, one supporting Robert Jackson and the other in favor of Hugo Black. Rumors swirled that each man had threatened to resign from the court should the other be named chief justice. Their contentious relationship undoubtedly influenced Truman to make a less polarizing choice, as he ultimately named Secretary of the Treasury Fred Vinson to be the chief justice. This development didn't sit well with Robert Jackson, who felt jilted by the development, especially with going outside of the current justices for the new chief justice, and his resentment toward Hugo Black continued to fester.

Justice Jackson eventually hit a boiling point and snapped, leading him to send a scathing rebuke of Justice Black to the Senate and House judiciary committee, in which he sensationally claimed that Black had engaged in "bullying" tactics and had threatened to declare "war" unless Jackson "covered up facts" pertaining to the *Jewell Ridge Coal vs. UMWA* case. Jackson went on to declare:

> *It is high time that Congress have the facts. If war is declared on me I propose to wage it with the weapons of the open warrior, not those of the stealthy assassin.*

Regarding Justice Black voting in favor of his former law partner Crampton Harris (the Jewell Ridge Coal case being the second time it had happened), Justice Jackson went on to say:

> *I wanted that practice stopped. If it is ever repeated while I am on the bench I will make my Jewell Ridge opinion look like a letter of recommendation by comparison.*

The brouhaha led to national news headlines, with Jackson's venomous remarks leading to descriptions of "bickering" among the justices and the Supreme Court being described as having "lost dignity" due to the situation that was said to be "without parallel in modern court history." The temperature eventually cooled between the two justices, at least publicly, but the situation was said to weigh heavily on Jackson, with many claiming his health suffered greatly from the incident. Justice Robert Jackson passed away from a massive heart attack at the relatively young age of sixty-two.

It is commonly known that working in the coal mining industry can lead to an early grave, but in at least this one case, coal mining apparently shortened the life of someone who never spent one minute underground.

III

LEGENDARY PLACES
OF SOUTHWEST VIRGINIA

St. Albans and Its Troublesome Past

In Radford, you can gaze across the New River to see a magnificent old building on the hill in the distance. The grand, ornate structure seemed to peer over the town with an eerie splendor. The locals know it as "St. Albans," and they know its stories. But an outsider may admire it from a distance without ever knowing it's known throughout the country by paranormal investigators as the most actively haunted structure east of the Mississippi River.

The lush land was once inhabited by Shawnee Natives until white settlers came into the area. Tensions rose between the two until the Shawnee attacked the settlers of the land, killing and capturing many members of the group. This land was part of the Draper's Meadow Massacre, where the legendary Mary Draper Ingles was seized. The bloodshed on this land planted the seeds of sorrow to come.

The building was fully structured in 1892 when a former professor at Emory and Henry College, George C. Miles, opened St. Albans' Boys School. The German teacher named the Lutheran school in honor of the famous St. Albans of England. The school was notorious for being very demanding on the boys, not only tolerating but also encouraging demeaning banter and physical bullying. The new boys were referred to as "rats." Nicknames were made up for each boy in a manner to attack physical flaws or effeminate attributes. Abuse ran rampant between the boys themselves and the faculty.

The abandoned St. Albans Sanatorium near Radford. *Melody Blackwell-West.*

Early years of St. Alban's Boys School. *McConnell Library Archives Radford University.*

A yearbook from the time gives an idea of this abuse by telling how one boy would not be returning to St. Albans in the fall. This was said to be saddening in the book, as the boy was often used as a human football on the grounds. That boy died at home at the age of eighteen in what is suspected as injuries from the abuse he endured at the school. In this toxic environment, it comes as no surprise that mental health issues arose. Boys started ending their own lives at the school. The raunchy reputation of the school continued, causing a drop in enrollment numbers. Finally, in 1911, the school closed its doors and ended the mistreatment of many students who suffered there.

The building didn't sit empty long. In 1915, it was purchased by Dr. J.C. King, who planned to reopen the establishment as St. Albans Sanatorium for the treatment of mental and nervous disorders. In 1916, the doors reopened as a mental hospital that would continue in operation until 1985. The hospital served a need in the best way it possibly could at the time. Patients were respected by staff and interacted with Dr. King's family, who lived on-site. Tenants worked in communal gardens on the grounds used to feed the entire unit with the freshest produce. Unfortunately, mental health was not as well understood in those days, which meant patients were often subject to damaging experimental medications and tactics such as electroshock therapy.

At one point, the sanatorium had only 48 members of staff compared to the enrolled 6,509 patients. With experiments, ignorance of mental health and these staffing shortages, the quality of life in the asylum declined and death tolls increased. One documented story is of a woman named Rebecca. Rebecca was admitted to the asylum while pregnant. Unfortunately, Rebecca gave birth to a stillborn baby, which she kept hidden in a jar in her closet. Nurses found Rebecca's lost child and confiscated the baby. Rebecca's grief and depression escalated to the point of her suicide. The attic bathroom in which Rebecca ended her life saw a total of twelve suicides throughout its time. It became known as the suicide bathroom. This area is a common hotspot for paranormal investigators, who often detect highly spiritual activity here.

Down the hall, a woman hanged herself by her sheets out an attic window. In the many years since this occurrence, the woman has been seen hanging from the same spot. Nurses doing rounds would spot the figure from the window and run to rescue the patient, only to find nobody there. Other figures are often seen, footsteps are heard throughout the building and objects will move with nobody around.

Third-floor bathroom known as "the suicide bathroom" at St. Albans. *Melody Blackwell-West.*

The grand staircase in the main lobby of St. Albans Sanatorium. *Melody Blackwell-West.*

On the ground floor, another area of high paranormal activity is the area known as the King Center, where Dr. King and his family resided. Movement is often heard in the area when nobody is around. A heavy tarp hanging over a doorway pulls away as if someone is pushing it to walk through, but that person is not seen. A young girl's singing has been heard from the grand staircase landing nearby.

In the basement sits a large and heavy metal safe. New owners stood in the vacant building talking of construction plans. These plans must have angered the spirit tenants. As the men walked away, they heard a deafening crash. Expecting to rush back into the area to find a ceiling collapsed, the safe that had been flipped upside down. Groups have attempted to flip it back over with no success.

Also in the basement is a boiler room where there is a spirit known as "Smokey." Smokey is said to have been a worker in the boiler room who liked to smoke. Cigarettes are often smelled in the area. Guests will leave unlit cigarettes in a tray in the room as a gift for this spirit.

One of the most gripping stories of St. Albans's spirits is the case of Gina Hall. Gina Hall was an eighteen-year-old Radford student who went missing

The bowling alley in the basement of St. Albans. *Melody Blackwell-West.*

Side view of St. Albans. *Melody Blackwell-West.*

in 1980. Her car was found later near St. Albans, with her blood in the trunk of the vehicle. Her killer was the first person in Virginia to be convicted of murder without the body of the deceased being found. Over thirty years later, some of Gina's remains have been found, but theories still run rampant in the area. With the killer having been rumored to work on the grounds of St. Albans, many believe Gina's body was brought to the boiler room of the sanatorium to be burned for easier disposal. Others believe part of Gina's body may be hidden somewhere on the grounds.

Part of these theories have led many to believe Gina's spirit resides in St. Albans. Many have said the mention of Gina's name in the bowling alley adjacent to the boiler room has produced a mist in the shape of a female. Many even believe a demon known as "red eyes" seen at St. Albans could have influenced Gina's killer. Paranormal investigators on the scene have picked up electronic phenomena believed to belong to both Gina and this negative energy.

The morgue of St. Albans Sanatorium is one of the least active areas of the building. It's suiting to be that way, as it's not dead energy throughout the building. The energy is so strong at St. Albans that it makes the building seem to be alive. A world continues inside when no living being is around. It is no wonder why it has been the subject of various TV shows and books. Any lover of ghost stories who wishes to see for themselves why this building is known as the most haunted location on the East Coast can plan a tour themselves. No fear of being alone inside, as no room is ever empty. If it's red eyes that happen to follow, though, it would be wise to bid the building farewell and leave as fast as you came.

MAJOR HAUNTS AT THE MAJOR GRAHAM MANSION

The spooky history behind the Graham Mansion began before there was a Graham Mansion, as there had previously been a log cabin on the spot where the home currently sits. The cabin was owned by a local man named Joseph Baker Sr., who was a slaveholder. According to legend, in 1786, two of Joseph Baker's slaves, Bob and Sam, were making moonshine and ended up "taste testing," which soon led to them becoming very intoxicated. The

Side view of Major Graham Mansion. *Melody Blackwell-West.*

Major Graham Mansion. *Melody Blackwell-West.*

two men then decided it would be a good idea to murder Baker for reasons that are still unclear. Some have said that there had been a deal where Baker had promised them freedom under some circumstances, which led to an argument that ended in the murder. Others say that Baker was perhaps a cruel master, and in their intoxicated state, the men snapped and decided to put an end to his life and rid themselves of his oppression.

Bob and Sam initially denied their guilt when they were arrested and questioned but soon confessed under interrogation and led the authorities to where they had buried Baker. According to the Montgomery courthouse records, the members of the jury trying the case were allowed to view Baker's corpse and reported, "His skull appears to be split open with an ax as witness our hands the 30th day of April 1786." Based on the evidence and their confession, Bob and Sam were pronounced guilty of the gruesome murder and sentenced to execution by hanging, which was carried out swiftly. It is said they were hanged from a tree on the property and their bodies buried on a hill overlooking the cabin, with some considering the location to have been chosen to serve as a reminder and a message to other slaves of their grim fate.

Top: Children's bedroom at Major Graham Mansion. *Shane Simmons*.

Bottom: Major Graham Mansion in Max Meadows, Virginia. *Shane Simmons*.

The ghosts of Bob and Sam are said to haunt the grounds to this very day. They manifest themselves in various ways wandering around the property, and there have been other claimed sightings of their lifeless bodies hanging from a tree in the yard, slowly blowing back and forth by gusts of wind.

The property was later purchased by the family of Squire David Graham, who built a new house over the same area where Baker's cabin had previously stood. The Graham family originally built a frame house on the property, but as they had more and more success in the business world, they continued to add on, leading to the majestic home that it finally became. Allegedly, Squire David had a reputation as a heavy drinker, and his wife, Martha, suffered from chronic depression leading to a troubled marriage. Martha's depression became so severe that she was often locked into a second-floor room of the house, where she would etch her name into the windows in an attempt to keep her sanity. These etchings can still be seen today.

One of the couple's sons, Major David Graham, is the namesake for the home and served as a lieutenant in the Confederate army. The attic floor of the house has a room with a secret panel that is called the "Confederate Room" due to stories that it was used for clandestine military meetings during the Civil War.

The home also possesses an upstairs room that was used as a classroom where Major Graham's sisters, Bettie and Emily, taught orphans and local children during the war. The most frequent ghost activity is from one of the children thought to have been taught there by the name of Clara. Clara was very close to Bettie Graham and received special treatment in the class. Unfortunately, Clara is said to have passed away at the age of seven from tuberculosis. One legend has it that she died during a snowstorm, so they kept her body wrapped up in a blanket in a closet of the classroom for several days until the weather improved enough for a proper burial. Clara is said to be a friendly ghost who has been known to frequently make her presence felt verbally. Some have even claimed that if she is feeling playful, you can roll a ball on the floor in the classroom and she will roll it back to you.

The basement of the house has a shackle room where disobedient slaves were sent for punishment. It has been rumored that Martha Graham was sent there on occasion when her depressive manias would get out of control. There have also been claims of EVPs (electronic voice phenomenon) where voices have been heard in the shackle room pleading for help. Paranormal investigators have had numerous experiences throughout the house and the entire property giving it the dubious distinction of being listed as one of Virginia's Top 10 Most Haunted Places.

The Major Graham Mansion is one of the few haunted properties that celebrates the spooky history attached to it and is open to the public for viewing. Every October, it becomes the Haunted Graham Mansion and converts to a haunted house attraction for the season in a display that will scare the pants off of anyone bold enough to enter.

THE OCTAGON HOUSE
AND THE MANY SIDES OF ITS STORY

A treasure of a historic home still stands tall in Smyth County despite years of emptiness. This treasure, however, is said by many to be a former center of terror, leaving behind tormented spirits. The Abijah Thomas

Early days of the Octagon House. *From* SWVA Today, *March 22, 2017.*

Octagon House is an enigma of sorts in the eyes of many—beautiful and captivating on the outside but dark and haunting on the inside.

This unusual house was built by slave labor between 1856 and 1857, just outside the town of Marion. Its designer was also to be its owner, Abijah Thomas. Thomas had a talented vision for business and industry, earning himself the title of the "foremost industrialist of Smyth County." The land his new octagon house was to be built on was only a small fraction of the ten thousand acres he owned by 1860. About a mile from his home along the Holston River, Thomas developed the Holston Woolen Mills. Around the mills developed a small town, Holston Mills, complete with its own post office, schools, factories and homes.

Thomas also developed a pig iron (also known as crude iron) furnace southeast of Marion. At the time, pig iron was in high demand for the Confederacy. Along with these establishments in Southwest Virginia, he owned a tannery and a cotton mill in Alexandria. Thomas had a good reputation in his time for the growth and resources he brought not only to Southwest Virginia but the whole state as well.

His creativity and contributions earned him attention and respect throughout the South.

Perhaps his reputation of being a visionary is how Thomas made the acquaintance of Orson Fowler, writer of the popular book *The Octagon House: A Home for All.* Fowler's book was responsible for a surge in octagon-shaped houses in America throughout the 1850s. It is said Fowler discussed the idea of Thomas building his own octagon house for better ventilation and better views from each room of the house. Thomas designed his own octagon-shaped two-story brick home complete with seventeen rooms, ten closets and a storage room. The homeplace was referred to as "Mountain View." The walls were strengthened by iron, and each of the six fireplaces was constructed with a piece of iron meant to help radiate heat. The bricks were made on-site by the enslaved.

The home was built incorporating several different styles popular for the time. The parlor was created to look like a marble temple, using a rare wall marbelizing technique typically reserved for official public buildings such as courthouses. Painted murals filled the walls of the home, where each room displayed a different color. Just shy of six thousand square feet, the home was a marvel for its time and is still the largest remaining octagon house in Virginia today. The elegance of the home for that area and time was unmatched.

Unfortunately, the toll of the Civil War and mismanagement of money put a stop to Thomas's industrial conquests. Many would say financial

More recent condition of Octagon House. *Melody Blackwell-West.*

Inside view of Octagon. *Melody Blackwell-West.*

Side view of Octagon House. *Melody Blackwell-West.*

mishandling was not Thomas's only flaw. While historical accounts speak well of Thomas, even saying many of his enslaved people stayed on to work for him after their freedom was granted, it is commonly said otherwise.

On the second floor of the eight-sided mansion was a center room without light called the "dark room." Many believe this was a room used by Abijah Thomas to beat and, in some cases, kill slaves he was not happy with. Red stains mark the floor in what historians say were caused by food spillage, but others claim it is blood. Many have spoken of seeing fresh blood run down the walls of this room as well. While it does appear this room was used for canned food storage, could it have been used for ulterior motives as well?

A terrifying angry spirit is said to accost many who made their way through the house to this center room, making anyone immediately run away in fear from the premises. The property has been plagued with reports of the sounds of tortured screams, cracking whips and moving chains as well as actual apparitions of ghosts. On December 1, the anniversary of Abijah Thomas's death, many have claimed to see a white-blue light making its way across the yard. This figure is believed to be Thomas himself.

A lot of paranormal activity is said to happen around the back of the house as well, where some claim a cellar once was. This cellar is also believed to be a focal point of abuse for Thomas's slaves. Many avoid this area or will only go with a religious artifact for fear of aggressive spirits. The now boarded-up windows were once said to be a window into the past with slave ghosts peering out. The current condition of this fear-invoking structure prevents further ghost investigations from locals but remains known as one of the most haunted homes in Southwest Virginia.

Whether or not there is truth behind the abuse of the enslaved people at Mountain View, no one in this time will know. But there is something to be said about a house that holds so much history. Both weddings and funerals were held in the home.

Abijah's funeral after his death at age sixty-two was held in his beloved home. At least one of his twelve children also was honored in death at the home. Strong emotions of love, joy, anguish and grief all took place in this rare structure. Certainly, some spirits may linger. But why it is haunted could be subject to debate.

The Octagon House was placed on the National Register of Historic Places in 1980 as well as the list of Virginia's ten most endangered sites list in 2015. An Octagon House Foundation has also been established to raise money for proposed restoration plans. The promise remains that this historic gem will get the renovation it deserves. One can only hope the remaining tenants of Abijah Thomas's octagon house feel the same way.

The Tragic Past of Ellenbrook Mansion

Stuart Land and Cattle Company is one of the oldest and most iconic cattle companies in the United States. The farmland dates back to 1774 when a man by the name of Henry Smith II started Clifton Farm in Rosedale. The land was granted to him by Patrick Henry as a reward for building an Indian fort along the Clinch River. Years later, when Smith's great-granddaughter Mary Taylor Carter married William Alexander "Alex" Stuart in 1849, she added a dowry of eighty thousand acres to Stuart's already large portion of land. That's how the whopping mass of farmland officially organized as Stuart Land and Cattle Company in 1884, named for Alex Stuart (brother of Confederate general J.E.B. Stuart) himself.

In 1858, a mansion was built in the stunning Elk Garden section of Stuart's farmland located between the Clinch River and Clinch Mountain. It was called "Number Four" for its number in the first Elk Garden phone system. After Mary's passing, Stuart remarried a woman by the name of Ellen Spiller Brown, and the new family moved into Number Four. Stuart renamed the mansion Ellenbrook for his new bride, though it was still often referred to as Number Four many decades after. It has also been called the Old Governor's Mansion, as Henry Carter Stuart, Virginia's forty-seventh governor and Alex's son, would have lived here years before building what's known as the Governor's Mansion just down the road.

From early on, Number Four had a reputation for being haunted. In the years not occupied by the Stuarts, the home was inhabited by other families linked to the farm. Several deaths are said to have occurred in the home or on the property. One was an unfortunate tragedy of a woman electrocuted talking on the new phone system in the home. A sick child is also said to have died in Number Four. People have reported seeing a ball bouncing and rolling in an upstairs room when no one was around, said to be the spirit of this child.

Farmhands and family died outside on the surrounding property as well. It's said one man who died in a horsing accident can still be seen on his

Ellenbrook Mansion in Elk Garden. *Melody Blackwell-West.*

horse on the grounds. With farm life, accidents can often occur and often did in Elk Garden. Which spirits were responsible for cold chills, a noisy kitchen, swinging doors and phantom voices all reported in the home we may never know.

For years, teenagers would explore the abandoned home, thrill-seeking a ghost adventure. Most would report strange activity of some sort, but whether the tricks were played by friends or spirits could be hard to determine. Thankfully, the home was restored by the Ratcliffe Foundation (founded by Smiley Ratliff), which now also manages a portion of the Elk Garden farmland. Now officially called Ellenbrook Mansion, the former home provides a mini museum of the Stuart family and also serves as an event venue. Although the appearance of Ellenbrook has been restored to its former bright and shining glory, it's safe to say the lingering energy has remained fully intact. Ellenbrook can help remind us that things are not always as they appear.

The Tavern:
Where Fine Dining and Frights Are on the Menu

Anyone who has spent time in Abingdon, Virginia, has likely passed by the building known as The Tavern. In a town chock-full of historic homes and buildings, The Tavern stands tall as the oldest commercial building still in use in Abingdon, having been built in 1779. Originally used as a tavern (hence the name), the building has served a wide array of purposes through the years, including an antique store, bakery, bank, cabinet store, general store, barbershop, private home and, these days, a restaurant. The town's first post office was housed inside an addition to the building, and the original mail slot is still visible. The third-floor attic of The Tavern even served as a makeshift hospital during the Civil War that treated both Confederate and Union wounded troops.

The Tavern has hosted numerous noteworthy guests, including President Andrew Jackson; President of France Louis Philippe; Senator Henry Clay; and Pierre Charles L'Enfant, the lead engineer in the planning of Washington, D.C. With that much life coming and going through its doors, it should come as no surprise that a spirit or two might take a liking to the building and decide to stick around.

The most commonly discussed ghost haunting The Tavern is the spirit of a young woman sometimes known as the "Tavern Tart." According to

The Tavern in Abingdon. *Shane Simmons.*

legend, the Tavern Tart was a popular prostitute or "lady of the evening," to be more polite, who was murdered on the second floor of the building by one of her clients. They had gone to her room to negotiate the terms of their "business" when something went terribly wrong. A loud crashing noise and screaming were heard by patrons downstairs, who rushed to see what was causing the disturbance. They soon discovered a gruesome sight before them. A young lady was lying on the floor. Her throat had been slit, and she was almost lifeless in a pool of her own blood. Her dying words were to gasp out the name of her killer, who had seemingly disappeared into thin air. A manhunt ensued, but her murderer was never found.

Her life may have had a tragic early ending, but she didn't let that stop her from keeping residency at The Tavern, as her spirit is said to reside in the building even today. Ever the flirt, she is known to be quite attracted to men despite her bad ending at the hand of one. She is said to pinch, grab or just give an old-fashioned slap to the rear of men she is attracted to in the building. It is quite the surprise for the men on the receiving end of her advances. The Tavern Tart has also been seen looking out the second-floor window deep in the night, dreamily staring down at men that capture her fancy in the street.

She isn't quite as fond of women patrons and will even show some old-fashioned green-eyed jealousy when an attractive lady threatens her reign as the belle of the building. She has been known to shove, pull hair and even throw objects at these female rivals. She seems to take special exception to pregnant women, giving them the harshest treatment for some reason,

Captain Gordon William Rife (*left*) and Stephen Alonzo Jackson (*right*). *The Tavern Restaurant.*

possibly because she never had any children of her own. Fortunately, she hasn't caused any real harm to anyone but has likely hurt more than a few feelings with her cattiness. The Tavern Tart is apparently more of a prickly rose than a shrinking violet.

Another ghost said to be roaming the grounds of The Tavern is that of Captain Gordon William "Captain Gord" Rife (also spelled Riffe). Rife served the Confederacy as a captain in Company B of the Twenty-Second Virginia Cavalry during the Civil War. He was shot dead on the property on May 18, 1880, by Stephen Alonzo "Lon" Jackson. An accomplished man in his own right, Jackson had been nicknamed the "Golden Hearted Virginian" and is credited for moving the Kappa Sigma fraternity into national prominence during his time at the University of Virginia. So, what would cause these two otherwise respected citizens to engage in a deadly gunfight?

Several potential motives for the murder have been floated throughout the years, but the most commonly accepted story is that Rife was the victim of the jealous rage of Jackson, who'd caught Rife cheating with his wife. An argument ensued between the men, with them eventually taking the dispute just outside The Tavern doors, where Jackson ended the matter, and Rife's life, with a bullet. Jackson is said to have then dragged Rife to the

Washington County Courthouse, where he left his lifeless body on the steps, reflecting that "justice had been served."

Pictures of both Rife and his murderer still hang on a wall inside of The Tavern, an acknowledgement of their significance in the history of the establishment. The ghost of Gordon William Rife is said to still roam the halls of The Tavern almost 150 years later. His ghost is thought to be less pleasant than that of the Tavern Tart, as he is known to be a little more aggressive in moving objects and causing commotion to let you know he is still very much present.

These days, the current staff and owner make it a point to clear the premises by midnight in a show of respect to the spirits that still haunt The Tavern. It would be wise for any patrons to pay respects as well to ensure that the bartender remains the only entity that ends up slinging drinks.

BURKE'S GARDEN: A VARMINT IN GOD'S THUMBPRINT

Burke's Garden is located in Tazewell County and is known far and wide as one of the most beautiful rural communities in the United States. The unusual bowl-like shape that forms the valley has been the source of debate almost since the area was first discovered. An aerial view of Burke's Garden would make it appear as if it could have been the result of a volcano cratering in the area. More recently, it is generally accepted that it was created by the collapse of limestone caverns underneath the area where Burke's Garden now sits.

Burke's Garden got its name most interestingly, according to legend. A local landowner named James Patton had contracted to have the land surveyed. One member of the surveying party was an Irishman named James Burke. Burke is said to have thrown away potato peelings while cooking a meal for the surveying crew while they were staying in the area. The following year, the surveying crew returned to the area, only to discover that potatoes were growing in the spot where Burke had thrown away the potato peelings. The men jokingly referred to the area as Burke's Garden, and the name has stuck ever since.

The area's beauty and fertile farmland have long attracted settlers of all types, dating back to the days when Indigenous peoples inhabited the area. These days, the primary residents have lived in the community for generations, and there's also a pocket of Amish families who reside there. Burke's Garden has been so highly regarded that George Vanderbilt II

Burke's Garden historical marker in Tazewell. *Shane Simmons.*

attempted to acquire the land before building his famous Biltmore Estate in Asheville, North Carolina. His overtures were rebuffed by the local farmers, who refused to sell their land.

Burke's Garden's lush fields also attract various species of wildlife, not always the desirable kind. The Burke's Garden Varmint was a mysterious wild creature that roamed Burke's Garden back in the 1950s, decimating the local livestock numbers. It is said to have killed well over four hundred sheep in its nearly year-long reign of terror—one farmer, Harry Lineberry, lost ninety-four sheep during the rampage. Residents were at a loss to stop the predator and were baffled as to what could be doing so much damage (estimated at over $32,000 worth in total—roughly $400,000 these days when adjusted for inflation). Wild speculation abounded as to the identity of the ravenous fiend, from a dog or wolf to more outlandish claims such as a kangaroo or baboon. The more time passed, the wilder the guesses began to get. Elaborate traps and other attempts to stop the killer were futile.

In February 1952, the desperate Tazewell County Board of Supervisors decided to contract with an experienced big-game hunter from Arizona, Clell Lee, to track down the menace. Lee arrived to a lukewarm reception from the local community but went about his business of finding out what had been the source of so much destruction. He soon discovered a track located inside a block of ice that indicated it was the work of a large coyote. The finding was quite surprising to residents, as there hadn't been a coyote sighting in the area before. Many remained skeptical.

Lee's trained dogs soon picked up on the scent of the coyote, and so the hunt began. Lee, along with the sheriff and other residents, headed out to find the animal and put an end to its killing spree. The first night ended without finding the coyote, but a determined Clell Lee insisted they start back out again the next morning at daybreak. The decision was somewhat controversial, as the following morning was a Sunday and local citizens had always held that was a day of rest and for going to church, not suitable for hunting.

The dogs soon found the scent of the coyote that morning and gave chase in a hunt that lasted for several hours. Finally, in a scene fitting for an old western movie, the coyote was found and shot dead in the Joe Moss Cemetery by a Burke's Garden resident named Alfred Jones. As you might expect, the coyote wasn't given a proper burial despite meeting his Waterloo in a cemetery. The Varmint was found to weigh in at thirty-five pounds and was four and a half feet in length with fangs extending for a full inch.

The "Varmint of Burke's Garden" mounted and on display at the Historic Crab Orchard Museum and Pioneer Park in Tazewell. *Justin van Dyke*.

The coyote was then hung from a tree just outside the local courthouse, where it was held on display for a good while with an estimated 7,500 people coming to view its body. A celebration dinner was held in Clell Lee's honor, and he became quite the local celebrity. The Burke's Garden Varmint was stuffed and now resides on display inside the Crab Orchard Museum in Tazewell, Virginia.

These days, the memory of the Burke's Garden Varmint is kept alive by a half marathon and 5k road race known at The Varmint held in Burkes Garden. Winners of the race receive a trophy in the form of sheep, a nod to the victims of the Varmint.

Hungry Mother State Park: A Historic Park with a Legendary Name

Ask any Smyth County native how to get to the closest beach, and you'll be given directions right to Hungry Mother State Park in Marion. A sandy beach on the 108-acre man-made lake with stunning mountain views is just one attraction at one of Virginia's oldest state parks. Visitors can also enjoy beautiful hiking trails, paddleboats, picnic shelters, overnight camping, cabins and yurts.

They even have an annual festival that boasts as the longest-running festival held in a Virginia State Park.

In June 1936, Virginia became the first state to open an entire state park system. Hungry Mother was one of the first six, which all opened the same day, and even hosted the official opening ceremony of the Virginia State Park System. Governor George C. Peery led the celebration, which thousands of Virginians attended. The family fun included concerts, a bathing beauty contest and a water pageant.

Hungry Mother State Park had been constructed by President Franklin Roosevelt's Civilian Conservation Corps (CCC), a voluntary work relief program for unmarried young men. The CCC was a relatively new program at that time, designed to help men having difficulty finding work during the Great Depression. The young men assigned to Hungry Mother State Park made impressively fast progress on constructing the park's five cabins, three shelters, a man-made lake and a beach. Today, the log cabins labeled as 1–5 are the original cabins built in the 1930s by the CCC. The park's three shelters, as well as the stone restroom facilities near Shelter 3, are all original structures. The park also pays tribute to the CCC with a special historic

View of Hungry Mother State Park. *Melody Blackwell-West.*

Early construction of Hungry Mother State Park. *Virginia State Parks.*

One of the original six cabins built by the CCC at Hungry Mother State Park. *Virginia State Parks*.

CCC Cabin road sign in Hungry Mother State Park. *Melody Blackwell-West*.

Marker for Molly's Knob Trail. *Melody Blackwell-West.*

walking trail and its parking lot medians, which are in the shape of different tools used to build the park.

As interesting as the history of the park itself is, the history of how the park got the name "Hungry Mother" is even more intriguing. The most told legend says Native Americans raided a settlement along the New River. Among the captives taken were a woman named Molly Marley and her young child. Molly managed to escape captivity with her child into the wilderness, where they were left to roam for days, searching for help.

As any loving mother would, Molly fed her child any berries they came across. Eventually, the hunger and elements got the best of Molly and she collapsed. Her child wandered along the creek until help was found, but all the child managed to repeat was "hunger mother." The search party found Molly deceased at the foot of the mountain we now know as Molly's Knob. The stream was named Hungry Mother Creek. As the land was acquired later for the state park's construction, the name of the park was chosen from the heart-wrenching legend that gave the creek its name.

While the history behind the name is a sad one, it's comforting to think of the families that have bonded and enjoyed the park for almost one hundred years now. Its construction during the Great Depression was a purposeful one: to bring joy and sanctuary to all, no matter the person's financial position. Hungry Mother State Park has done just that for Southwest Virginia and beyond. The three pillars of this park could even sum up the spirit of Southwest Virginia: a mother's love and sacrifice, the labor of hardworking men and determination in times of deep hardship.

BARTER THEATRE: SO GOOD YOU MAY NEVER WANT TO LEAVE

Robert Porterfield was born on December 21, 1905, in the town of Austinville in Wythe County. Coming from an affluent family, Porterfield had opportunities not afforded to many other children and young adults in the area, including the opportunity to get a college education. He attended Hampden-Sydney College for a couple of years, but his real passion became theater once he was bitten by the acting bug. He dropped out of college and moved to New York City to pursue his dream of working in acting and the theater.

Robert Porterfield returned to manage the family's real estate holdings following the death of his father. Despite the change in circumstances, he

The Barter Theatre in Abingdon. *Melody Blackwell-West.*

never lost his passion for the theater. He was determined to establish a repertory and doggedly pursued the endeavor. He chose to begin the venture during what, on the surface, would be the worst time to launch such an endeavor, the heart of the Great Depression.

Porterfield established the repertory that would become the Barter Theatre in downtown Abingdon, Virginia. The Barter first opened on June 10, 1933, which placed a financial hardship on potential ticket buyers struggling under the strain of the Great Depression. Robert Porterfield hatched the idea of easing that burden by allowing residents to bring in produce and livestock to trade for the tickets, which is where the theater earned the name "Barter."

His bartering theater proved to be wildly popular locally and eventually grew to national prominence.

In the early years, the town jail was located right under the stage, giving a new meaning to the phrase "captive audience." Another footnote, the building also once served as the fire department, and until 1994, a siren was attached to the top of the building. The actors were instructed that if the alarm went off, they were to freeze in place until the siren was cleared, and then they would resume the play exactly where they'd left off.

Numerous well-known and much-respected actors got their start at the Barter Theatre, including Gregory Peck, Ernest Borgnine, Patricia Neal, Ned Beatty, Larry Linville, Hume Cronyn and Gary Collins. Even Wayne Knight, who portrays the insufferable Newman on the wildly popular sitcom *Seinfeld*, and Jim Varney, the infamous Ernest P. Worrell of *Ernest Goes to Camp* and *Ernest Scared Stupid* fame, spent time perfecting their acting craft at the Barter.

For his part, Robert Porterfield continued to dabble in acting during the early years of the Barter Theatre. His biggest film role was as Zeb Andrews in the massive film *Sergeant York* starring Gary Cooper, a multiple Academy Award winner and the highest-grossing film of 1941.

Robert Porterfield maintained his role as artistic director of the Barter Theatre from the repertory's opening until his death in 1971. The name Robert Porterfield will forever be associated with the Barter Theatre, and some say his spirit has never left. The most lasting and persistent haunting associated with Barter Theatre is that of the ghost of Robert Porterfield.

Several actors have claimed to have seen the ghostly figure of a tall man wearing a gray suit quietly pacing back and forth in the balcony during rehearsals and at other times when no one else should have been in the theater. The ghost isn't threatening or particularly scary but more of a comforting entity that is simply watching over the "baby" he created.

The Barter Theatre was officially named the State Theatre of Virginia in 1946 and remains a great venue for world-class productions and world-class fun for a night on the town; however, you may want to leave the livestock and vegetables at home, as they prefer cash or credit cards these days. Robert Porterfield was famous for giving an opening speech before each show that ended with him saying, "If you like us, talk about us. And if you don't, just keep your mouth shut." We would like to borrow that saying for this book.

The Lyric Theatre: You're in for a Scream!

In the beautiful college town of Blacksburg is the historic Lyric Theatre. Though the theater first graced Blacksburg as early as 1909, it wasn't until after "talkies" (movies with sound) started becoming popular in the late 1920s that the current theater on College Avenue was built. Construction was completed on the new theater with a full sound system in 1930, but not without tragedy. When history and drama combine, the stories that result can really be a "scream."

When the doors first opened on the new Lyric Theatre in April 1930, it was considered a luxury movie-watching experience. It was even one of the first theaters in Virginia to show pictures with sound. The theater had a seating capacity of nine hundred, leading-edge technology and much-envied air-conditioning. The family of one of the original three founders eventually took over management of the theater and it remained a family-run business until 1989.

The Lyric Theatre in Blacksburg. *Jimmy Smith/Spooky Appalachia.*

In 1996, the theater reopened (though it had still been in operation for venue rental in the previous years), and in 1999, the theater celebrated its grand reopening after extensive renovations. Thankfully, the theater has been able to keep up with advances in technology and stay open as an icon of Montgomery County. Despite all the changes to technology and structure, the Lyric has had some inhabitants from its very start.

During the theater's construction, a man fell to his death from the upper wall of the building. For decades, the story was told that the phantom noises heard primarily in a back stairwell belonged to that deceased construction worker, but only half believed. The incident, however, was said to be a confirmed fact by a relative of the deceased to a theater worker. To know the stomping of footsteps up and down the stairs at strange hours may truly belong to a life lost in tragedy is enough to give chills to any witness.

As if a ghost who mutters, stomps and invokes cold chills is not enough to bring a shriek, there is another spirit occupant of the theater who does the shrieking herself! Theater employees have been witness to the loud shrieking of a woman seeming to come from the theater lobby. The female cry is so shrill, it is said to sound like a screaming banshee. Presumably, the same spirit is also said to scream, "Let me out! Let me out!"

It is believed the woman once was an occupant of an apartment atop the theater, but any other details remain unsolved.

Part of the fun of Southwest Virginia folklore is the questions only answered in imagination. Southwest Virginia is fortunate enough to be home to so many historic icons such as the Lyric, but the theater really holds its own in thrilling stories. Whether you are a fan of mystery, horror or drama, the Lyric can meet all your needs before the movie even begins. The absolute best part? You can watch a movie with company beside you without ever having to share your popcorn.

HONAKER HIGH SCHOOL AND THE PRINCIPAL WHO NEVER LEFT

High school principals have serious and difficult jobs. The best ones often get extremely attached to the community, the students and the school itself. When it comes time to move on, it's not always so easy for many. In the Redbud Capital, it's often believed this was the case for former principal A.P. Baldwin.

A. P. BALDWIN, Principal

Left: Former longtime Honaker High School principal A.P. Baldwin. *From the* Torch.

Below: A.P. Baldwin Gymnasium beside Honaker High School. *Melody Blackwell-West.*

Honaker High School main building. *Honaker High School.*

Arda Palmer Baldwin, known as A.P., was an Emory and Henry College graduate who kept a close watch over Honaker High School from the start of his tenure in the early 1940s until his retirement in 1976. A.P. Baldwin was an administrator admired and respected by staff, students and parents. He won many educational awards for his service to the developing minds of Russell County. The high school's gym was even named A.P. Baldwin Gymnasium when it was dedicated in 1971 in honor of the man who oversaw the high school for over thirty years.

After the death of A.P. Baldwin in 1981, some strange occurrences started happening in the school, primarily the gymnasium, which many claimed to be caused by the former principal. A.P. was a known smoker, so it was natural when people started smelling and even seeing smoke in the hallways with no one around for the witnesses to believe that to be the spirit of A.P. The smoke is sometimes described as cigarette and other times as cigar and would often appear in the basement and stairways of the gymnasium, where A.P. was known to frequent. There are also numerous reports to this day of doors opening on their own, knocks, footsteps and even apparitions of a broad-shouldered man smoking in the gym's basement hallway.

Another repeated complaint of fright comes from what is now used as the band room in the main building. Students have shared experiences of ghostly apparitions and doors opening with no one around. This spirit is typically thought to belong to someone other than the beloved former principal, but who it could be is unknown.

Not every teacher or principal leaves an impression on their former students. It speaks volumes about A.P. Baldwin's dedication to Honaker High School that he would still be talked about decades after his passing. The question of his lingering presence at the school is a curious subject for most students and even some intrigued visitors. A.P. may still be teaching a valuable lesson in life and the afterlife to all he encounters at Honaker High School.

THOMPSON CREEK TUNNEL: A THRILL-SEEKER'S DREAM…OR NIGHTMARE

A late-night drive looking for some frights, like teenagers and amateur ghost hunters both do in these small communities, may lead to an eerie tunnel in the Thompson Creek area of Honaker. Around a bend in the road, it comes into view, standing tall with the creek running through one side and a road that often floods on the other. Train tracks run overtop in a wooded area, maybe unknown to anyone not familiar with the region unless a train happens to be going by.

These late-night thrill seekers often drive to the center of the tunnel, roll the windows down and turn off the headlights to show their bravery in this test of the spirits. In the cases where no one is grabbed from the car or happens to see a ghost, the driver heads on out for a cruise through town until the next time someone is feeling up to being scared. These midnight ghost adventurers are one reason to take caution when going through the tunnel. Another is that visibility to the other side may be limited as you enter. A third reason is the actual ghosts themselves.

The story most often told says an enslaved man from adjacent Buchanan County escaped his enslavers. A group was formed from the neighboring county and pursued the man to the Honaker area, where he was captured. He was taken to this nearby tunnel and hanged there as punishment for his pursuit of freedom. Many years later, a brother and his younger sister living close by were playing in the creek by the tunnel when the little girl's ankle was caught. Unable to get loose, her brother ran home for help. When he returned with an adult, the little girl was nowhere to be seen. In the place where she had stood was a single shoe left behind.

Thompson Creek Tunnell. *Melody Blackwell-West.*

Inside view of
Thompson Creek
Tunnel. *Melody
Blackwell-West.*

A rescue party was put together to search for the young girl but to no avail. The child vanished into thin air. Many said the spirit of the man who met his end in the tunnel years before had taken her as revenge. Some even said his spirit must have been what held her in the water until she was left alone.

For generations, this story has been told with no one truly ever knowing what happened to the girl. Arguments could even be made that the whole story was made up to keep kids cautious when playing in the creek. But how long can a story with no basis in truth withstand verbal recollection? It all remains a mystery. As for thrill seekers visiting the tunnel, that's guaranteed.

What Haunts Hollins University?

Hollins University has a long history dating to 1842, when it was first established as Valley Union Seminary. It became Hollins Institute in 1855 and has served as an institution of higher learning ever since. Any public institution that dates back well over a century has likely acquired a few spirits that have decided to hang around, and Hollins University is no exception. Hollins University is routinely ranked in the top ten most haunted colleges/universities in the United States. There are several haunting tales associated with the school, but one seems to consistently stand out above the rest.

These days, this haunted activity manifests itself in the form of piano music coming from the building that houses the music programs at the university, Presser Hall. Presser Hall was built for the college's (Hollins University was Hollins College from 1911 to 1998) music program and was dedicated on March 31, 1926. Presser Hall was named for the college's one-time director of music, Theodore Presser, a renowned name in the field of music during his lifetime. Presser was known for his keen attention to detail as well as his philanthropy. Perhaps some of that passion for quality was developed during his teenage years in Pennsylvania, spent molding cannon balls for the Union army during the Civil War.

Testaments to Theodore Presser's reputation for exception and things that stand the test of time are evident even today, almost one hundred years after his death in 1925. The Theodore Presser Company is still in existence as a music publishing and distribution company with roots that date to 1883. Presser Hall remains a major part of Hollins university's music department and campus life. Finally, in some quarters, it is also said that Theodore Presser's spirit still haunts his namesake building, his ghost being another vestige of his life at Hollins and his attachment to things that last.

Presser's ghost is said to occupy the second floor of Presser Hall, where several practice rooms and offices are located. There's even a bronze bust of Presser that sits prominently atop a large pedestal on that floor. Hollins University students have taken to decorating the bust in various manners using T-shirts, hats, sunglasses and such. His bust strikes a rather stern pose, so the decorations serve to take the edge off. The lightened mood doesn't appear to have dissuaded Presser from making his presence felt in other ways.

Fortunately, the ghost of Theodore Presser has a reputation for being harmless and even kind. He is most often said to be heard playing the piano when no one else is on that floor or in the building, usually later at night, as passersby walk past Presser Hall. He will occasionally cause a bit of a

Presser Hall at Hollins University. *Hollins University.*

commotion, however, if he is disturbed in the evenings, as he seems to enjoy his quiet time or—ever the perfectionist—if a student hits a sour note. It could be considered comforting to know that Presser is still emotionally invested in Hollins after all this time.

In contrast to the story of Theodore Presser, another haunt that is said to roam Presser Hall is one born out of a tragedy. Another common ghost story attached to Hollins University and Presser Hall is a tale of unrequited love. According to legend, a male music teacher at Hollins became smitten with one of his gifted young female students. Bewitched and smitten with her talent and good looks, the teacher succumbed to feelings of love for the young pianist.

Despite his best efforts to fight what he knew to be an inappropriate attraction, he felt he could no longer hold back so he cornered her in a passionate embrace in the hopes the feelings were mutual. As he went to kiss her, to his embarrassment, the young lady rejected his advances, leaving the professor crestfallen and desperate to save his pride. These feelings of rejection combined with the fear that she would report his overly aggressive and brutish behavior led him to snap and kill her by strangling her with a piano wire.

The young pianist's ghost is said to still haunt Presser Hall, and the piano playing that is often heard outside the building late at night is often attributed

Theodore Presser at work in his office. *Internet Archive, https:// archive.org/details/ EtudeOctober1923/ page/n6/mode/1up.*

to the young lady who is said to have perished at the hand of her music professor. Perhaps she is practicing her skills on the piano to make beautiful music in the hopes it will make up for her life ending on such a sour note.

THE HISTORICALLY HAUNTED MARTHA WASHINGTON INN

One of the grandest luxury hotels in Southwest Virginia also holds a fascinating and haunting history. The Martha Washington Inn and Spa has served many purposes in its time, the most recent being an upscale hotel with a spa, restaurant and boutique. Since its construction in 1832, it's also been used as a private residence, a women's college and a Civil War hospital. The deeply rooted history of this magnificent structure has led to many chilling tales being told of supernatural occurrences.

Better known locally as the Martha, the building was originally constructed as a private residence for the prominent Preston family. General Francis Preston, son of Draper's Meadow Massacre survivor William Preston, and his wife, Sarah Buchanan Preston, built the lavish home for less than $15,000. The center brick structure of the present-day building made up the Preston home for the couple and their nine children. The Preston family living room now serves as the main lobby, and the hotel boasts of keeping much of the integrity of the original details of the home.

In 1858, the Preston family sold the home for $21,000 to the United Methodist Church to become a women's college. The school was given the name Martha Washington College in honor of the well-respected first lady. It wasn't long, however, before the school had to take on the new roles of training barracks and hospital for the tragic War Between the States. The grounds became training barracks for the Washington Mounted Rifles, which were under the command of J.E.B. Stuart. The girls at the college had to serve as nurses for both Confederate and Union troops, with battles between the two happening just outside the doors. Many deaths occurred in and around the Martha during the Civil War, which is believed to be a large factor in making this one of the most haunted hotels in Virginia.

One of the most popular stories from this time is about one of the schoolgirls who was working as a nurse and her beloved Confederate soldier. The girl's devotee was said to have been assigned an important mission of delivering papers with the whereabouts of the Union army to General Robert E. Lee. The soldier knew the risks of his mission and couldn't bear to leave without telling his beloved goodbye. He snuck through an underground tunnel to the Martha and up a stairway to get to his girl, but as they were meeting,

The Martha Washington Inn and Spa in Abingdon. *Melody Blackwell-West.*

two Union troops discovered him and shot him dead. The young soldier lay dying in his lover's arms, bleeding out onto the carpet below. Since this tragic day, the carpet has been replaced several times, yet a bloodstain always seeps back through. The floors underneath were also refinished, but the blood always returns as a reminder of love lost.

This tragic Civil War love story was not the only one belonging to the Martha. One of the young women caring for soldiers at this time was a kind soul named Beth. The girl loved to play the violin and often would play for those she was caring for.

One Union soldier in particular loved to hear Beth's violin, and eventually, the two fell in love. Unfortunately, the soldier's injuries were beyond care, and he died in the room now known as number 403. Beth played a low Southern song for her deceased soldier in a tribute to their love. Only three weeks later, Beth passed away from typhoid fever. Since her passing, many have still heard Beth's sweet violin playing coming from room 403.

The ghosts of the Civil War that linger at the Martha aren't limited to soldiers and their lovers.

One of the most commonly seen spirits around the grounds is a horse. There have been many reports over the years of a horse running free around the Martha. Being in the center of downtown Abingdon, this can be an alarming event. The most alarming part, however, is that the horse vanishes into thin air. It's said this phantom horse dates back to the Civil War when his owner was shot down on the property. The horse left in the tragedy still roams, avoiding the attacks of war and searching for his owner.

In the years after the Civil War, the Martha was prosperous, with renovations adding the upper story with dormers to the center building. In 1913 and 1914, the three-storied east hall and two-storied west hall were added to the property. These major renovations proved to be too much of a financial burden, and in 1919, the college was forced to merge with Emory and Henry College. The consolidation was not enough to keep the college going, and in 1932, it was closed.

Thankfully, the property was revamped as a hotel a few years later and opened for business in 1935. Since then, the hotel has hosted several prominent figures such as Eleanor Roosevelt, Presidents Harry Truman and Jimmy Carter and Elizabeth Taylor. Part of the success of this historic hotel is credited to the proximity of the Barter Theatre. Being just across the road, the Martha was used for years to house actors and actresses being featured at the Barter Theatre, including Patricia Neal, Ernest Borgnine and Ned Beatty.

For added convenience, there is even an underground tunnel running from the Martha to the Barter.

This tunnel is home to another infamous spirit. Despite its infamy, this spirit is not as well understood as the others at the Martha. What is known is this spirit is a dark and angry one. Anyone who has felt this spirit while passing through the tunnel has complained of the ominous feeling the presence projects. Some feel this spirit belongs to a man who was killed in the tunnel during a collapse in 1890. Others believe it is another spirit tied to the Civil War.

Not many other facilities still stand with as much history as the Martha Washington Inn. Fortunately, with major restorations performed in the 1980s, the Martha became a landmark of history, adding to the beauty of Abingdon. Its role in the Civil War was a significant one, not only then but also now as a part of the town's history and folklore. It's without question why some spirit guests choose to stay.

PATRICK HENRY HOTEL: WHERE GUESTS WOULD CHECK IN BUT SOME WOULD NEVER LEAVE

Hotels and motels seem to be a hotbed for paranormal activity, and Southwest Virginia has no shortage of these haunted hospitalities. Like people, these buildings accumulate their unique history and experiences over time—a lot of happy memories but, occasionally, tragedy. Those tragedies often turn into hauntings when a customer checks into a room but their spirit decides to never leave.

The Patrick Henry Hotel in Roanoke was once a luxury lodging destination in the area and played host to numerous upscale events and gave a good night's rest to several prominent guests. Time has moved on, and the parties are over these days. The hotel isn't even a hotel anymore, having transitioned into luxury apartments and retail space. The guests have all checked out and moved on with their lives except for at least one guest that is said to have never left the building. This guest is said to be the spirit of a young flight attendant that lost her life in a most gruesome manner in the 1980s.

According to legend, the young lady checked into room 606 for some well-deserved rest after a long day of flights that ended at the Roanoke Regional Airport. She checked into the hotel and was never seen alive again outside of the building. The day after she arrived, the maid sent to clean the room made a grisly discovery. Entering the room, she saw blood everywhere: the

The Hotel Patrick henry in Roanoke. *Postcard.*

bedsheets, the floor, the wall and so on. Horrified, she followed the blood trail to the bathroom where she saw found the naked bloody body of the young lady lifeless in the bathtub, a victim of multiple stab wounds. She fled the scene, screaming for help in her panic. The police were summoned, and an investigation was launched to solve the brutal murder. As the young lady had no local ties and no known lover, it made the case exceedingly difficult to solve. Was she the victim of a random, heinous act? Had she met someone in the hotel bar that led to a bad outcome? The crime was so vicious that police strongly suspected it to be the work of someone that knew her, but who and why? So many questions and so few answers. Due to the precious few clues and plausible theories, her murder was never solved.

The trail of the killer went cold, but the ghost of the young lady stayed very active. In the following years, several similar stories were told by different people who would have had no way of knowing the other versions. Repeatedly, a scene was described where the ceiling of the room opened up, revealing a wrought-iron spiral staircase with a dark-haired female apparition descending from it. The ghost is said to be comforting and friendly, but that is not always well-received, despite the nonthreatening nature. There have also been several claims of dark vibes and cold feelings near the closet of the room. It is suspected that the killer had hidden in that closet before pouncing on his young victim.

The killer may never be found, and maybe that is why the ghost of the young flight attendant lingers in the building of the former Patrick Henry Hotel. Patrick Henry famously said, "Give me liberty, or give me death!" so it isn't unreasonable to think the young lady may be lingering to symbolically say, "You gave me death, now give me justice!"

HILLTOP MOTEL: A NIGHT OF FRIGHT IS NO DELIGHT

Unlike many other hotels and motels with rich histories of hosting the rich and famous, the Hilltop Motel in Doran has had a more inglorious history by comparison. It has been in a state of decline since the late 1960s and earned more of a reputation as a "no-tell motel" where trysts can take place for an affordable price. It has also long been rumored as a spot where illicit drug activity has occurred. As might be expected, the seedy reputation has led to several bad outcomes, including a few mysterious deaths. Overdoses and the occasional heart attack brought on by "overstimulation" have led to the demise of a few guests. It should come as no surprise that this has also led to many reports of paranormal activity.

One example of these mysterious deaths was the passing of the mayor of a neighboring state that occurred while he was meeting up with a much younger woman for a negotiated night of passion. According to legend, the combination of alcohol and excitement of the rendezvous was more than his aging heart could handle, and he was found expired in the bed of his motel room. His young lady friend had skipped out and relieved his wallet of its cash in the process. Perhaps his spirit roams the grounds of the Hilltop Motel.

There have been numerous reported sightings of apparitions in the motel rooms, where guests have felt the presence of someone beside their bed when no one else was there. Strange noises as well as television sets and lights

The Hilltop Motel in Doran. *Shane Simmons.*

flickering on and off have been noted. Tales of a locked door opening and shutting while the guest is in the bathroom have been told. Some have even said that they've felt the touch of unseen hands while staying at the Hilltop. They often refer to politicians as "glad-handers" and "back-slappers," so maybe it is the work of the small-town mayor after all.

The whole point of a no-tell motel is secrecy, and there's an old saying, "Dead men tell no tales," so it should come as no surprise that we may never know the true meanings or the people behind the paranormal activity that takes place at the now-defunct Hilltop Motel.

THE RESTING TREE: A PLACE OF PEACE

A slave's day was an excruciatingly long and difficult one. Not all would have a place of escape or refuge for peace and rest. Thankfully, those on the Preston Plantation (formerly known as the Walnut Grove Plantation) in Bristol, Virginia, had their place of occasional solace. The Resting Tree was what they called the large oak tree on the property east of the Preston home.

The Preston Plantation was named for Robert Preston, an Irish immigrant who moved to Washington County in 1779. In 1780, he became the first surveyor of Washington County. That same year, he was married and acquired almost eight hundred acres of land, which he named Walnut Grove. The house he built on the property in the 1790s is one of the oldest remaining structures in Washington County.

By the 1830s, the Preston family had around thirty slaves laboring on the property. Those that worked in slave labor on the property would frequently

seek shelter under the mighty oak's shade. During daily work breaks, they would spend time with their children here. They would rely on the tree's strong trunk when their weakness felt too much.

In 1798, an enslaved child named Dan was welcomed into glory. His loved ones chose his final resting place to be in the most peaceful spot they knew, beside their beloved tree. Several years later, in 1803, an elderly man named Reuben was also laid to rest underneath the oak tree. After this burial, it officially became a burial site for the enslaved

Opposite: Historical marker for the Resting Tree in Bristol, Virginia. *Melody Blackwell-West.*

Above: The Resting Tree in Bristol. *Melody Blackwell-West.*

Plaque for the Resting Tree in Bristol, Virginia. *Melody Blackwell-West.*

of the Preston Plantation. Not much else is known of those who were laid to rest beneath the tree, as there were no formal records, and only three graves remain intact now. There are, however, several limestone markers surrounding the Resting Tree to signify burial spots.

The area around the Resting Tree continued to be used as a cemetery throughout the 1800s.

After slavery was abolished, it remained in use as a holy ground for the Black community. Around 2010, the road beside the site was named "Resting Tree Drive" in honor of the sacred space. A marker was also placed at the site, telling the story of how the Resting Tree got its name.

Stepping into the vicinity, one could see why this would be the place of choice for peace and quiet in a life full of hard labor and sorrows. The air almost feels lighter and easier to take a deep breath. The environment invites you in like a parent welcoming a child home from war. The tree itself beckons you in with its limbs like a mother's kind embrace. The birds seem to sing a softer, more uplifting song. The energy of the area is more still and tranquil than its surroundings in an almost supernatural way.

There are only glimpses into the lives of the enslaved at the Preston Plantation. Perhaps the Resting Tree was nature's compensation for the cruelty of man to those enslaved. A glimpse of heaven in a harsh life. Now, it may serve as a remembrance to those who were set free only when laid to rest beneath the mighty Resting Tree.

IV

LEGENDARY CREATURES, WITCHES AND OTHER CREEPY CHARACTERS OF SOUTHWEST VIRGINIA

THE BLACK SISTERS OF CHRISTIANSBURG

Long before Disney ever introduced us to the movie Hocus Pocus or the three Sanderson sisters, there were three sisters believed to be witches unleashing havoc right here in Southwest Virginia. The darkness of these sisters, however, would put the Sanderson sisters to shame.

Virginia Wardlaw, Mary Snead and Caroline Martin had family ties to Christiansburg but didn't move to the area from Tennessee until around 1902, when Virginia started running the Montgomery Female Academy. Virginia's widowed sisters, Mary and Caroline, helped run the boarding school for girls. It didn't take long for the whispers and stories to start circulating around town.

After all, these women drew a lot of mystery and attention. They dressed all in black, even wearing heavy black veils, earning themselves the nickname the "Black Sisters." The sisters also rarely came out during the day, and when they did, they would cross the street to avoid interacting with locals. One late-night trip they often made was to visit the cemetery in town.

Students spoke of strange behavior by the sisters, such as finding them huddled in the middle of the night, murmuring and making ritual-like gestures with their hands. One story still told is that a young woman at the school became pregnant while attending the academy. As if this didn't draw enough negative attention at the time, once the baby was born, it was never seen, and the young mother would never speak on the matter. The

Montgomery Female Academy. *Montgomery County Historical Society.*

general belief was that the sisters got rid of the baby by throwing it into a well on the property.

Incidents that were seen and heard of were enough to give the sisters the reputation of being witches, but things really got heated when Mary's son, John, came to town.

John Snead had been sent for by the sisters to be a groundskeeper at the school. On his train ride into town, John "fell" from the train but was rescued just in time. Many say John so dreaded joining his mother and aunts, knowing their nature, that his "fall" was no accident at all. Several weeks after arriving, John had another close call, this time falling into a well. It was said to be a believable accident for small children or animals, but a healthy grown man was another story. He nearly drowned but was pulled out by a gentleman in town before it was too late. Had John reached his limit with his mother and aunts or was there some sort of witch's curse on the young man?

Just a week after John's second brush with death, students were awakened to the sounds of a man's screams. The girls ran to the source of the screaming to find John on fire and writhing in pain on the floor. He soon after succumbed to his severe burns. The story told by Virginia was that poor John must have accidentally knocked a candle over onto himself in his sleep, but that didn't explain how his entire body was charred. Upon further investigation, it was found John's bedclothes had been soaked in kerosene and that John's mother and two aunts had taken a hefty life insurance policy out on John a week before his untimely death. It was widely believed the Black Sisters were behind his demise, but no solid proof was formed to hold a conviction.

With tragedy and suspicion swirling around the boarding school, attendance understandably plummeted. In 1908, the school closed after fifty-six years of operation. The sisters had blown through John's life insurance money and fled to New Jersey, where they again found themselves in a scandal.

Caroline's daughter, Oceana "Ocey," and Mary's son, Fletcher, had married one another despite their family's disapproval. When the sisters learned Ocey was expecting her first child, they became overly involved in the couple's lives, even demanding they live with them. Fletcher and Ocey's daughter was born but died shortly after. Ocey became pregnant again the following year. For reasons still unknown, Fletcher left and was believed to be dead by his expecting wife. In reality, Fletcher had fled to Canada and changed his name, leaving Ocey behind.

Ocey's health deteriorated as time went on living with her mother and aunts. Ocey was said to be a beautiful and kind girl, which may explain why she seemed to be a target of torture by the sisters. Multiple accounts stated Caroline had withheld food from her daughter from the time she was a small child. During her second pregnancy, she was found to be emaciated and very sick by a doctor who pleaded with the sisters to provide food for Ocey, which they claimed they could not afford. The sisters wanted the doctor to inform Ocey she was nearing death and convince the twenty-four-year-old to create a will. Instead, the doctor sent a nurse to care for Ocey, but the sisters refused the help. Ocey's second child was born sickly and was taken by the sisters to an orphanage, where he later passed away.

Months later, Virginia made a call to the police one afternoon telling them an accident had occurred and to please send a coroner. When the doctor arrived at the home, he was greeted by Virginia in her normal black garb and heavy veil. The home was unkept and did not appear to be lived in.

He was led to an upstairs bathroom, where he found the body of young Ocey Snead in the bathtub, her head turned toward the faucet and a hand still grasping a washcloth. A note was found lying with her clothes; it appeared to be a suicide note left by Ocey, stating the pain of losing her two children was too much to bear. When questioned, Virginia stated she hadn't checked on Ocey all day, as she had told her that morning that she wished to be left alone. This set off alarm bells to the doctor, as Ocey's body had apparently been in the water for at least twenty-four hours.

1.—Ocey W. Snead, the victim. | 3.—Fletcher W. Snead, husband of | 5.—Miss Mary Snead, the third
2.—Miss Virginia Wardlaw, aunt of | the victim, Ocey W. Snead. | Wardlaw sister, who is the mother-
the murdered woman, and the first to | 4.—Miss Caroline B. Martin, mother | in-law of the victim, is also under
be placed under arrest. | of the victim and who is under ar- | arrest in connection with the crime.
| rest in connection with the crime. |

Ocey Snead (*top left*), Virginia Wardlaw (*top right*), Caroline Martin, Fletcher Snead and Mary Snead (*bottom left to right*). *Wikimedia Commons.*

An autopsy and a formal investigation were performed. The young woman was found to have died by drowning and was near starvation, with morphine also being detected in her system. Multiple suicide notes were found claiming to be by Ocey but not matching her handwriting. The home where Ocey was found was not actually being lived in by the sisters.

The three sisters had also taken out several life insurance policies on the young woman. Horrifically, there were also remains of an infant found in the sisters' furnace. The evidence found in 1909 led to murder charges against the sisters, with Caroline, Ocey's mother, believed to be the mastermind of killing Ocey for insurance money.

Mary Snead was released on a technicality and lived out her remaining days with her son in Colorado and then California. Caroline Martin pleaded guilty and was sent to an insane asylum, where she passed away years later. Virginia Wardlaw starved herself to death while in jail awaiting trial. Virginia's body was buried in Christiansburg with only a broken, weathered stone marking her final resting place at Sunset Cemetery.

The full extent of the crimes of the Black Sisters is unknown, with rumors of Mary killing her husband and seven-year-old son years before the deaths of John and Ocey. While the ladies' reign of terror came to a halt in New Jersey, a legacy of horror still follows them in Christiansburg. Many believe their spirits, as well as the spirits of their victims, still linger.

Broken headstone of Virginia Wardlaw. Her parents' headstones can be seen in the background. *Melody Blackwell-West.*

Broken headstone of Virginia Wardlaw in Christiansburg, Virginia. *Melody Blackwell-West.*

It was a common belief throughout Christiansburg that the Montgomery Female Academy building was haunted after the reign of the Black Sisters. There were reports of a baby's cries coming from a well on the property, as well as the sound of a man's screams coming from the building. Many say random fires would break out in the building, apparently out of nowhere. Eventually, the county purchased the property and demolished the building. In 1935, a new building was erected in its place to be used as first the Christiansburg High School and eventually Christiansburg Middle School. Although it was a completely different building, these schools also had a notoriety for being haunted.

With Christiansburg's mascot being the Blue Demons, the school had a demon face painted on a gym wall that was said to have a tear of blood running from its eye. Cold feelings, floorboards creaking and even black shadow-like figures were seen throughout the building. Students refused to go to certain parts of the school alone. Today, the lot is vacant; another middle school was built in a different location.

A lot of attention also goes to Sunset Cemetery, where many believe Virginia Wardlaw's grave resides. Ghost hunters and paranormal enthusiasts frequent the broken stone that marks the spot of her body, where many say you can also spot dark figures or stir up cold chills and uneasy feelings. Like many killers, the true extent of the evil of the Black Sisters is buried with them. The impression left on the Christiansburg area, however, lingers on.

THE BIG STONE GAP VAMPIRE

Every horror fan loves a good vampire story, but not many of these originate from Southwest Virginia. This story is a rare tale, sure to leave you a little pale, and has been told for over one hundred years now. To make it even more shocking, it takes place in the sleepy little town of Big Stone Gap in Wise County.

In the late nineteenth century, Big Stone Gap was flourishing because of its coal and iron-ore facilities. People had hopes of it becoming the "Pittsburgh of the South" for industry and growth. Immigrants were coming into Southwest Virginia from all over for the prospect of good jobs and better lives. Despite this, it was still a tight-knit community where people looked out for one another.

Because of this, townspeople grew suspicious when a prominent farmer started to find his cattle dismembered and drained of blood. Animal attacks happened but never anything like this. There started to be talk of what or who could have been responsible for such violent acts that had the potential to damage a farmer and his family's livelihood. That's when the townspeople started watching Rupp a little more closely.

Rupp was a strange fellow who had come to Big Stone Gap from somewhere in Europe. He kept to himself out in the cabin in the woods he had built on his own. Rupp had shown up in town shortly before these mysterious incidents started occurring. Could it be possible there was something more sinister and subhuman about this out-of-towner?

A couple young boys decided one day to spy on Rupp, no doubt having heard talk around town about the mystery surrounding him. Like young, mischievous boys are known to do, they wanted to see for themselves to get their blood pumping. What they saw, however, could not have been expected. Peering through the windows of Rupp's cabin, the boys saw him sitting in front of his fireplace, gnawing at the raw leg of a cow. The boys ran back to town, breathlessly telling the adults what they had seen.

The townspeople went to the sheriff, demanding Rupp's arrest. But on what grounds? The sheriff denied their demands, telling the townspeople just because Rupp was eating raw meat, there was no proof that a crime had been committed. Shortly after this incident, the town drunk disappeared. He was found a few days later in the woods near Rupp's cabin. Just like the cattle, he had been dismembered and drained of blood. Not long after, a traveling salesman failed to report to his home office, leading to a search. He, too, was found dead in the woods, dismembered and drained of blood, just like those before him.

The townspeople had had enough. They were convinced their odd European newcomer was behind these tragedies and if the sheriff wouldn't handle it, they would. A group went to Rupp's house, but no sign of him was around. Finally, one brave soul decided to try the door. The group went into the cabin and, to their horror, found body parts belonging to man and beast strewn throughout his home. His kitchen was covered in blood.

A search party was launched to find Rupp and punish him for his crimes while a fire was lit in the small cabin. His home was destroyed, but Rupp himself was never found. To this day, it's said both animals and humans are known to disappear from the area in the woods Rupp once lived.

As for the basis in truth, we may never know. No records can be found from that time in Big Stone Gap to back up this story of a blood-sucking immortal creature. It can be quite common, at least in today's time, for popular destinations trying to grow to omit repelling information from their news. In any case, it pays to be cautious in the woods of Appalachia, or else you may not leave the same way you entered.

Sin-Eaters

Imagine your day to meet your maker comes and your loved ones lay bread upon your chest to absorb the sins of your lifetime. A stranger comes in, says a few ritual lines and eats the bread to take on your burden. It may sound very strange, but this was actually a common practice for centuries that lingered on in Appalachia longer than its countries of origin. The practice is known as sin-eating, and it may surprise you to know just how recently this ritual was performed in Southwest Virginia.

Sin-eating was an Appalachian tradition passed down from the immigrants of Wales and Ireland. Although there is documentation of different variations throughout the world even earlier, the practice of sin-eating became popular in Wales in the eighteenth and nineteenth centuries. As a large population of Welsh and Irish immigrants made their way into the Appalachian Mountains, they brought these same rituals with them. Many believe old pagan beliefs and behaviors mixed with the Catholic beliefs of absolution led to the practice of sin-eating. Many people would fear their dying loved ones had unrepented sins, and so the job of the sin-eater was created.

Most often, it was bread placed on the chest of the dying. Bread was believed to be the best absorber of sins from the body, but sometimes an ale was included or another item of food altogether.

Typically, sin-eaters were people who were poor and anxious for an opportunity for a meal and a small amount of money. A sin-eater may have also been a person who felt their soul was damned to hell already, as sin-eaters were believed to be bound to these sins for all of eternity. Because of this belief, sin-eaters were usually outcasts who had to live in isolation, shunned from their community. Townspeople would often refuse to look them in the eye and could also be rude and disrespectful. They were seen as a necessary evil. Despite this, there are also accounts of sin-eating being a family business. Sins would be passed down from father to son as part of a generational curse. Each job completed would make the sin-eater that much more wicked in the sight of these believers. However, some Appalachian sin-eaters remained anonymous, wearing a cloak and hood to protect their identity. This anonymity made it possible for a sin-eater to even be able to have a family.

The practice became obsolete in the ancestral lands of Wales and Ireland around the turn of the twentieth century, but traditions die out slower in the hills and hollers of Appalachia. Sin-eating is said to have remained a fairly common practice in isolated areas of Appalachia well into the 1950s. Reports of sin-eaters lingered even into the 1970s in some Southwest Virginia counties, such as Wise and Dickenson.

No matter what your beliefs are on the absolution of sins, surely everyone can agree that sin-eating is better left off the current job market.

Granny Witches

In the deep hollers and dark valleys of Appalachia lie many mysteries. Appalachian folk magic is one of those mysteries, leaving many questions to those unfamiliar with the practice. It is a crucial way of life for those living in the remote hills, and most people in Southwest Virginia have at least heard of some of these ancient customs.

Appalachian folk magic, often referred to as granny witchcraft, is a long-held tradition brought over from European settlers and blended with Native American and African American customs. The Appalachian Mountains have always been a remote area, but even more so in the early days of settlers. There typically was very little access to doctors and other necessary services.

The people, primarily women, of Scotland, Ireland and England, therefore used the folk magic and healing rituals of their native lands. As they blended with the Indigenous people, they taught the settlers about the native plants and their useful properties. When Germans migrated into the area, they also learned these ways and added to their own customs. As the African people were brought over as slaves, they too taught others in the Appalachian Mountains their knowledge.

In a blend of faith healing, folk magic and superstition, these granny witches would use herbs, plants, moon phases and Bible verses to heal or cure almost any ailment or concern. Communities relied heavily on granny witches for healthcare, delivering babies and guidance. Dowsing was one method used by granny witches to find groundwater. The individual would hold a forked stick or a pair of rods and walk along the location in question. When an adequate supply of groundwater was underneath, the stick pointed toward the ground or the rods would cross. It is believed in this practice that the water seam produces a force that causes a reaction to the tool being used.

People called on granny witches for love advice or guidance in decisions. Sometimes they would be given a cup of tea for the granny witch to read the tea leaves left in the bottom of the cup as a form of divination. Some of these granny witches were even able to scry, or see the future, in a bowl of water or through quartz or other crystals. Often the cure for an ailment would come from the granny witch's kitchen or garden. Dried basil was placed over doorways, windows and fireplaces to prevent wicked spirits from entering. Raw radish or mustard was placed under the pillow of a person plagued with bad dreams. For a child with respiratory issues like asthma, a sourwood stick was measured to the length of the child. When the child outgrew the stick, it was believed the respiratory ailment would also be outgrown.

Despite these practices being seen as general witchcraft by many, it was not considered so in this area. This Appalachian folk magic was an important piece of survival in isolated regions such as Southwest Virginia. Christianity was foremost in the lives of most who practiced it. This type of healing could be reinforced by scripture, and many Bible verses were used in healing. One verse commonly used still today is Ezekiel 16:6, which reads: "And when I passed by thee, and saw thee polluted in thine own blood, I said unto thee when thou wast in thy blood, Live; yea, I said unto thee when thou wast in thy blood, Live." (KJV) This verse is said to stop blood flow in the event of hemorrhage or any other unnatural or unstoppable flow of blood.

In the practice, many were believed to be born with special powers. For instance, the seventh son of a seventh son, a man who has never seen his father or a person born with a veil of skin over their face were all individuals believed to have unique abilities. These individuals were, for one, believed to be able to cure thrush in a baby by breathing in its mouth. Payment was not typically expected, but those wanting to show their appreciation to the granny witch would often give some type of food.

Traditions and folk magic knowledge are still being actively passed down from generation to generation though not practiced as often. These ways have faded with the development of technology and resources, but many do remain. Outsiders may not understand, but if you've been in Southwest Virginia a good length of time, you've probably witnessed a little magic.

Appalachia's Bigfoot

Southwest Virginia is a hotbed for stories and sightings of extremely large, hairy, bipedal creatures, all with a human-like appearance that are said to roam these hills and hollers. They've been given different names from Woodbooger to the Beast of Gum Hill, but they all relate to eerily similar tales of Bigfoot, Sasquatch and the Yeti. The earliest sighting of such a creature dates to the mid-1800s, making it one of the oldest claims in the country. Virtually every county in Southwest Virginia has a story of these creatures, but the two towns that yield the most sightings are Norton and Saltville. The Woodbooger of Norton and the Beast of Gum Hill near Saltville are the most recognized stories in the region.

High Knob is a popular destination for folks in the Norton and Wise County area, as it's known for having spectacular views from atop a lookout tower located there. High Knob is part of Stone Mountain and possesses a lot of majestic scenery in all four seasons. Depending on the time of year, you can see beautiful green hillsides in the summer, gorgeous foliage in the fall, a snow-covered mountainside in winter and the colorful blooms of springtime. In addition to these opportunities, it is said that if you are there in the right place at the right time, you just might encounter a Woodbooger roaming the woods.

The descriptions of Woodbooger are very much in line with those familiar to Bigfoot—tall, hairy, ape-like and possessing an extremely pungent odor. There are often comparisons made to Chewbacca of *Star Wars* fame, although Chewie would likely take offense to it, as the Wookie appears to be a little more well-groomed and stylish, not to mention sociable.

These cryptid sightings have been claimed in the area for years, so much so that parents used to tell their children not to go out in the woods lest a Woodbooger grab them. While the cryptid was initially used as a tool to incite fear, more recently, the folks in the Norton area have embraced and even celebrate the history of the Woodbooger. They've gone so far as to declare the Flag Rock section to be a "Woodbooger Sanctuary." Fortunately, Woodbooger hasn't been said to pose any apparent danger to locals. He is quite the local celebrity and even has a statue erected in his honor at the trailhead in the park at Flag Rock. This Appalachian Bigfoot is even active on social media, as "official" Woodbooger accounts have been made for Facebook and Twitter to help market the story. Woodbooger T-shirts are big sellers in the area, and there have been multiple television series that have come to the area to try to catch a glimpse of him on film. There's even a local restaurant named in his honor.

The Beast of Gum Hill is another such creature that is said to roam the Saltville area on into Washington County. The description is very similar to the Woodbooger, with witnesses claiming to see a figure approximately seven feet tall with a reddish or dark brown coat of thick hair. This creature is thought to be drawn to the town by the vast salt wells in the area that have long been known to bring in all manner of life, from mastodons to woolly mammoth, for the much-needed mineral. It stands to reason that if a Bigfoot were to exist, it would eventually make its way to Saltville.

A viral YouTube video from the area titled "The Beast of Gum Hill" elevated interest in and awareness of Bigfoot in the area to new heights. It even lured in the camera crew from Animal Planet's *Finding Bigfoot* series to go on a search for it. The show didn't conclusively prove or disprove the validity of the video, but it did inspire other Bigfoot enthusiasts to come to the area in their search for the truth. The town of Saltville hasn't seemed to have embraced this reputation as much as Norton, but maybe another sighting or two would change that situation.

There is no scientific evidence to support the existence of the Woodbooger, the Beast of Gum Hill or similar creatures, and many sightings can be explained by misidentification of known animals, hoaxes or other natural phenomena. However, legends and stories of these mysterious creatures continue to persist throughout Southwest Virginia, and they remain a popular topic of folklore and cryptozoology. They are some of the most widespread and lasting tales in the area, so it isn't likely that they will end anytime soon. It would be fair to say that if stories of another creature are to surpass these tales of Bigfoot, it would have some mighty big shoes to fill.

THE BEE ROCK TROLL

There has been a rise in tales of frightening creatures in the woods of Appalachia at night. Stories of unseen figures calling out to people, luring them into the dark for their sinister motives. The story of the Bee Rock Troll is just one example of these creatures coming out not only at night but during broad daylight too. It's a reminder that what should be feared the most is the unknown.

In the late 1800s, when coal was king in Southwest Virginia, towns were booming to life seemingly overnight. There weren't enough local men to fill the demand for work within the coal mines and the rails used to transport it. Many people moved from other countries to fill the void in hopes of better lives. When the Cumberland Valley Division of the Louisville & Nashville (L&N) Railroad started constructing a line between St. Louis and Tidewater Virginia, it was decided the best route would be by creating a tunnel through a rock fault in Stone Mountain. It was then, in 1891, the town of Appalachia sprung to life.

The Bee Rock Tunnel was formed as a connection that runs between the towns of Appalachia and Big Stone Gap. Ripley's "Believe It or Not" once labeled the tunnel as "the world's shortest railroad tunnel." Though it wasn't the actual shortest, at forty-seven feet and seven inches long, it was one of the shorter railroad tunnels used for not only coal but also U.S. Mail, passengers and baggage.

During the construction of the tunnel, workers would trade out areas of work day to day, resulting in many hands involved in the production. Before long, accounts started flooding in of a short, stocky creature that seemed to live in the woods and caves of the area. Everyone that saw it noted the ugliness of the small, suspicious being.

Because of the workload, workers would camp along the Powell River at night only to be awakened by a shrill voice coming from the woods saying,

Above: Bee Rock Tunnel in Big Stone Gap. *Postcard*.

Left: Bee Rock Troll statue at the head of the Powell River Trail in Appalachia, Virginia. *Melody Blackwell-West*.

Powell River Trailhead in Appalachia, Virginia. *Melody Blackwell-West.*

Bee Rock Troll statue at Powell River Trailhead. *Melody Blackwell-West.*

"Come help me, please come help me." Generally, these men had either seen or heard tell of the troll-like creature and were afraid to go off into the woods alone at night. It had never been determined whether the troll was friendly or menacing, and the men were not about to figure it out in the middle of the night.

As late as the 1950s, there have been reports of the grotesque creature being seen in the woods around the Bee Rock Tunnel. A family living nearby would report hearing cries for help from the woods at night. Rail workers would also report seeing the creature dart across the tracks ahead when passing through the area. The train operated through the Bee Rock Tunnel until 1987, and the tunnel is now in use as part of the Powell River Trail.

So many questions have been left unanswered about the Bee Rock Troll, at least by any witnesses left to tell about it. With no eyewitnesses since the late 1950s, one could reason the troll has long gone from the area. If you happen to hike along the Powell River Trail, you just may want to think twice about how you answer a call for help from the woods.

V

UNEXPLAINED PHENOMENA AND OTHER LEGENDS AND LORE

Fairy Stones

The legend of fairy stones is both gripping and magical. For any who are not familiar, fairy stones are crossed-shaped staurolite crystals found within the ground. They can be found in various formations in a few places throughout the world, including Brazil and Sweden, but never quite the perfect cross or as plentiful as what they are in and around Fairy Stone State Park in Patrick County.

The legend of how the stones were formed is an old one, passed down from the Cherokee. It says that when the Earth was young, there were spiritual beings we know now as fairies. The fairies gathered in our Appalachian Mountains, singing and dancing, until one day a messenger was sent from a faraway land. This messenger was an angel that appeared to the fairies to tell them of Christ's death. As the fairies heard of Christ's crucifixion, their tears fell to the ground, forming these cross-shaped stones as they hit.

The Cherokee believed these stones were gifted to those of pure heart and that they would give them special powers. Appalachians throughout the years passed down superstitions of the stone's abilities, including protecting its owner from the curse of a witch. It's still believed by many today to be a talisman of good luck or protection.

Because of the stone's abundance in the area, the name fairy stone used as the name of one of the original six Virginia state parks. Geologists say the stones were originally formed about seven miles below the Earth's surface. As the Blue Ridge Mountains ascended, the crystals formed blocks that were

An example of different variations of fairy stones. *Virginia State Parks.*

turned into cross shapes as they rose toward the surface. Once the crystals are at ground level, natural elements wash away the softer surface to uncover the perfect cross shape.

Fairy Stones can be found in three variations of the cross symbol. The first is the Roman cross, which is the most commonly seen symbol of the cross. The second is the St. Andrews cross, a cross in the shape of an X. The last is the Maltese cross, which is formed by four intersecting V shapes. The Maltese is the most sought-after among fairy stone hunters, as this is the rarest form.

Visitors of Fairy Stone State Park are welcome to hunt their own fairy stones, but only without the use of tools. It's said that the best way to find these hard-to-spot earth-colored stones is by looking around tree roots, as they are more likely to be weathered away in those areas. And if you are lucky enough to find your very own fairy stone, you just may want to treasure it, just in case those old legends stand true.

THE MYSTERY OF DR PEPPER

The Dr Pepper soda boasts of having twenty-three flavors, but the story of its origin seems to have even more than that. One origin story, even the name

Dr Pepper itself, is linked to the Southwest Virginia town of Rural Retreat. While the company claims it started in Waco, Texas, locals to Southwest Virginia believe otherwise, and with good reason.

The drink is said to have been created in the 1880s by a Brooklyn-born pharmacist named Charles Alderton while he was working at Morrison's Old Corner Drug Store in Waco, Texas. Alderton had been schooled in England, which included training in carbonated beverages. Alderton and his boss, owner of Morrison's Old Corner Drug Store, Wade Morrison, mixed carbonated water, fruit juices and sugar to create an unusual concoction. The drink was originally called a "Waco," but as the soft drink grew in popularity, it required a more official name. That is when the drink first became labeled "Dr Pepper." How it got that name, however, can cause quite a debate.

Around 1874, Wade Morrison was hired by Dr. Charles T. Pepper to work in his medical office and pharmacy out of Rural Retreat. Dr. Charles T. Pepper was a well-respected man, serving the healthcare needs of all of Wythe County. He gained his degree from the University of Virginia in 1855. Later, he served as a Confederate surgeon at Emory and Henry College during the Civil War, while the college was being used as a Confederate hospital. As he established his business in Rural Retreat, he became known for mixing mountain herbs, roots and seltzer into tasty drinks. No doubt making the mixing of his recipes part of Morrison's job duties. This is why many people believe Wade Morrison stole the recipe for the popular drink while working under the beloved Dr. Charles T. Pepper.

Others believe Morrison chose to give the drink the name "Dr Pepper" as a way to honor his former employer, perhaps even the man who inspired him to create his own fizzy and delicious drink. Other stories say Morrison named the drink after his horse named Pepper. The "Dr" part was only added to the name to make buyers feel it was a healthy choice.

The drink became a major success in Waco. Morrison met a young beverage chemist by the name of Robert S. Lazenby. Together, Morrison and Lazenby created the Artesian Mfg. & Bottling Company in 1891, which was later renamed the Dr Pepper Company. In 1904, the World's Fair came to St. Louis and so did Morrison and Lazenby. They shared Dr Pepper with almost twenty million people, and the rest is history. Dr Pepper Company is now known as the oldest major manufacturer of soft drinks and syrups in the United States.

The company itself claims to have received dozens of stories of how Morrison came up with the name Dr Pepper, but they stand by none of them. Many in the town of Rural Retreat requested the town's water tower be painted like a Dr Pepper can as a tribute to the town's doctor, Charles T. Pepper, but the company rejected the request. Why was Charles Alderton given the main credit when Wade Morrison was the one to see it through? Perhaps to distance the beverage from Dr. Charles T. Pepper? Surely residents of Rural Retreat would recognize Morrison's new creation as being the same distinct, unique and favorite local recipe of Dr. Charles T. Pepper's? It could be said it was only a similar recipe Morrison created from the idea of Pepper's drink, but if Alderton is given the main credit for creation, that theory must be dismissed.

Too many questions surround the recipe and name of the Dr Pepper drink for any one story to be claimed as true. The world may never know Dr. Charles T. Pepper's true influence, but many Rural Retreat locals will stand by their belief that the beverage was created here in Southwest Virginia. It goes to show when you have a brilliant idea, stake your claim then and there, or else you may just land in a sticky situation.

The Legend of Swift's Silver Mine

The story of Swift's Lost Silver Mine is one of the great legends and mysteries in Appalachian history. The story dates to 1760, when an Englishman named Jonathan (also known as John) Swift is said to have discovered a large silver mine inside a cave in the Appalachian Mountains. The location of the mine has been the subject of much debate, research and speculation for over 250 years with no conclusive answer. The mountains of Eastern Kentucky and Southwest Virginia have been the most frequently rumored locations of the mine and the buried treasure.

The legend is based on a journal written by Jonathan Swift that claims he was led to a cave filled with silver ore by a man named George Munday. Munday had allegedly been held captive by the Shawnee Indians, where he'd learned of the vast silver deposit. Another variation of the story claims that Swift discovered the cave while pursuing a wounded bear. Swift's journal goes on to claim that he went to the cave for nine years mining the silver, then later burying some of it in other locations throughout the area. In 1769, Swift finally ceased mining and barricaded the cave due to the threat of Indian attacks and internal conflict between Swift and his crew. Before he could return to the mine, Jonathan Swift is said to have gone blind and spent his final years in Bean Station, Tennessee. Upon his death, Swift is said to have left his journal along with a map describing the location of the mine to his caretaker, a widow known as Mrs. Renfro.

Jonathan Swift's journal gives descriptions that are somewhat generic and could apply to almost any town. For example, some of the treasure is said to have been buried "by the fork of a white oak" and "in the rock of a rock house." Another reason for the uncertainty of the location is that there have been numerous variations of Swift's journal produced over time, creating further confusion. Jonathan Swift himself is the subject of much debate and speculation. Swift has been cast in different roles as a pirate, explorer, Indian trader, and counterfeiter. Some stories claim that Swift murdered his crew at the end of their last excursion in the heat of greed and was cursed with blindness, preventing him from ever relocating the mine. There has been some speculation as to whether or not Jonathan Swift even existed, as there is little historical data to prove his life. One of the first people to discuss Swift's Silver Mine was Kentucky author John Filson, who was known for his writings about Daniel Boone. Some historians feel that Filson wrote the journal of Jonathan Swift as a work of fiction, having been inspired by the novel *Gulliver's Travels* by the Irish author coincidentally named Jonathan Swift.

Many people have searched in vain for the lost silver mines, while others have been rumored to have found the mine or, at least, some of the treasure that Swift had hidden. The most notable was Dickenson County, Virginia resident Solomon Mullins, known as "Money-makin' Sol" and "Counterfeitin' Sol," who was well known for his counterfeiting operations. Mullins mixed pure silver with other metals to produce his phony currency, leading many to wonder how he'd been able to get that much pure silver. Although Money-makin' Sol never revealed where he got his silver, many locals speculated that he'd found it in one of the caves near Pine Mountain in what is now Clintwood. There is still a section known as Sol's Cliff in the area in his honor.

Like any good mystery, the story of Swift's Lost Silver Mine leaves more questions than answers—where is the mine located? Was there ever really a mine? If so, why hasn't any substantial silver ore been found in the area? Did Jonathan Swift exist? Whether you believe there is a Swift's Lost Silver Mine is up to each individual, but it still makes for a fascinating story.

The Baby House of Grayson County

In the secluded hills of Grayson County sat a cabin many decades ago known as the "Baby House." An older couple had several children, all daughters and all within childbearing years. And childbearing they did. Each daughter had multiple births, and each time the baby would disappear. Rumors started circulating in the community that the father of the grown daughters was "taking care of the issue" behind the house. Times were hard, and in the case of unwed mothers living at home, another mouth to feed was seen as a burden for her parents.

Patches of fresh dirt would be left in the yard of the cabin. As those would disappear, new patches would appear. Reports of babies crying at night started coming from the lawn of the old cabin. Neighbors would say it was the cries of the babies whose lives were stolen and now lay resting in the yard. Some could argue the story untrue, but why the crying continued long past the cabin being emptied and even torn down was a harder point to make.

Revenge of the Cats

Many religions believe that you reap what you sow; basically, what you put into the world comes back to you. Witnesses to one man's death in Grayson County would surely argue this to be true. There lived a man in the early 1900s who truly hated cats. Any cat that crossed his path was sure to meet a painful demise. His brutality shocked and terrorized many, but he never showed remorse for his wrongdoings.

As the man grew into old age, so did his wickedness toward animals, until the day come of his own demise. The man's family gathered around his deathbed to see him shrieking in pain. Scratches appeared on his body as he screamed, "They're coming for me!" The man howled in agony through a long-lasting death as the tormenter became tormented. The story was repeated from the family to neighbors and friends. The community had a new respect for life and charity as the man's death only served as a reminder to always treat others as you wish to be treated.

A Bad Egg

In Appalachia, granny witches have always played an important role in the survival and success of families living poor and remotely. These individuals given the nickname "witch" are a far cry from wicked beings full of hate in their hearts. Unfortunately, a world of evil does exist, bringing pain and hardship to others. For many years in previous centuries, these wicked beings who brought cruelty to others in supernatural ways were what most considered to be a witch.

One matron of a Grayson County family found herself answering the knock at the door of one of these suspected wicked witches. The witch asked the woman of the house for a couple of eggs from the family supply, which the mother of the house denied. Being a wife and mother during the Great Depression, her primary focus rested on making sure her hardworking husband and many hungry children were fed. The female neighbor, however, did not understand and left the property scorned and muttering.

The following morning, the matriarch of the family went to gather eggs, only to find all her chickens had died. Her belief until her dying day was that a curse had been placed on those chickens in retaliation for the denied request. The woman never returned, but the impression she left was a lasting one. As the old saying goes, don't count your chickens before they hatch, or don't depend on something before it happens. Had the witch been familiar with this saying, perhaps all heartbreak could have been spared.

BIBLIOGRAPHY

Allen, M. "A Culture Extra: Hollins University Shares Ghost Stories." *Roanoke Times*, October 31, 2012.

Anne, S. "Legend of the Fairy Stone." Virginia State Parks, April 11, 2016. https://www.dcr.virginia.gov.

Archer, B. "Region Laments Passing of Entrepreneur 'Smiley' Ratliff." *Bluefield Daily Telegraph*, November 2, 2007.

Atwood, A. "All Because One Man Had a Dream." Virginia State Parks, August 18, 2015. https://www.dcr.virginia.gov.

Bearak, B. "Feisty Virginia Millionaire Finds Escape Isn't for Sale." *Los Angeles Times*, March 5, 1984.

Best, Gary Dean. *Witch Hunt in Wise County: The Persecution of Edith Maxwell.* Westport, CT: Praeger, 1994.

Bristol Historical Association. "Robert Preston Home." https://www.bristolhistoricalassociation.com.

Busic, Janice. "Molly Tynes: Did She or Didn't She? SHE DID!" SCV Camp 840, November 30, 2006. http://scv840jb.tripod.com.

Chandler, Susan. *The Life of Charlie Fields.* Self-published, n.d.

Colonial Ghosts. "Haunted Roanoke." August 15, 2017. https://colonialghosts.com.

Department of Conservation and Recreation. "History of Virginia State Parks." https://www.dcr.virginia.gov.

Des Moines (IA) Tribune. "Chameleonic Patter Cited in Wage Lawsuit; Litigants Flopped, Not Judge Picard." February 18, 1947.

———. "Napoleon Hill…Has a Fortune to Share with You…If You Are Ready for It." January 31, 1956.

Duvall, James. *Mary Ingles and the Escape from Big Bone Lick.* Boone County Public Library, 2009.

Ely, Macel, II. *Ain't No Grave: The Life & Legacy of Brother Claude Ely.* Dust-to-Digital, 2010.

Fenneman, Nevin M. *Physiography of Eastern United States.* New York: McGraw-Hill Book Company, 1938.

Fort Worth (TX) Star Telegram. "Powers Given Ten Years, with First Three in Prison." August 19, 1960.

Hill, Napoleon. *Think and Grow Rich.* Chicago: Combined Registry Company, 1937.

Historic American Buildings Survey, C. (1933) *Abijah Thomas House, Thomas Bridge Road, Marion, Smyth County, VA. Marion Virginia Smyth County, 1933.* Documentation Compiled After. [Photograph] Retrieved from the Library of Congress, https://www.loc.gov.

Ingles, Colonel John. *The Narrative of Col. John Ingles.* Transcribed by James Duvall, M.A. Boone County Public Library, 2008.

Kinney, Pamela K. *Haunted Virginia: Legends, Myths, & True Tales.* Atglen, PA: Schiffer Publishing, 2009.

Kneebone, John T. "Allen, George Edward." In *Dictionary of Virginia Biography*, vol. 1. Richmond: The Library of Virginia, 1998.

Lee, A. "Martha Washington Hotel." Society of Architectural Historians, *SAH Archipedia.* https://sah-archipedia.org.

Leslie, Louise. *Tazewell County.* Radford, VA: Commonwealth Press, 1982.

Lingeman, Richard. "How to Lose Friends and Alienate People." *New York Times*, August 13, 1995.

Lost Colleges. "St. Albans School." https://www.lostcolleges.com.

Lucier, Armand Francis. *French and Indian War Notices Abstracted from Colonial Newspapers: 1756–1757.* Vol. 2. Bowie, MD: Heritage Books, 1999.

Lyric Theatre. "Brief History of the Lyric Theatre." https://www.thelyric.com.

Marion (AL) Times Standard. "The 'Fighting Allens.'" May 17, 1912.

Martha Washington Inn and Spa. "The History of the Martha Washington Inn and Spa." http://www.themartha.com.

Matzko, J. "Rescuing Bugs and Cursing Towns: The Eccentricities of Robert Sheffey." *BJU Today*, July 3, 2020. https://today.bju.edu.

Mays, Ryan S. "The Draper's Meadows Settlement (1746–1756), Part II." *Smithfield Review*, 2015.

McNeil, J. "Three Sisters and Their Haunting History." *Roanoke (VA) Times*, October 27, 2004. https://roanoke.com.

Montgomery Museum of Art and History. "205 College Street." https://montgomerymuseum.org.

New York Times. "Posses Close in on Allen Outlaws." March 24, 1912.

Octagon House Foundation. "Restoration." http://www.smythoctagonhouse.org/home.html.

Ogden (UT) Standard-Examiner. "Barter Theatre Opens in South." June 13, 1933.

Orgill, Michael. *Anchored in Love: The Carter Family Story*. Old Tappan, NJ: Fleming H. Revell Company, 1975.

Pendleton, William Cecil. *History of Tazewell County and Southwest Virginia: 1748–1920*. Richmond, VA: W.C. Hill Printing Company, 1920.

Portsmouth (VA) Star. "Floyd and Claude Allen Die for the Hillsville Massacre." March 28, 1913.

Powers, Francis Gary, and Curt Gentry. *Operation Overflight*. London: Hodder and Stoughton, 1971.

Powers, Francis Gary, Jr., Keith Dunnavant and Sergei Khrushchev. *Spy Pilot: Francis Gary Powers, the U-2 Incident, and a Controversial Cold War Legacy*. Amherst, NY: Prometheus Books, 2019.

Price, Charles Edward. *The Mystery of Ghostly Vera and Other Haunting Tales of Southwest Virginia*. Johnson City, TN: Overmountain Press, 1993.

Raymond, Jack. "Powers on His Way Home after Spy Swap with Reds." *Courier-Journal* (Louisville, KY), February 11, 1962.

Richmond Times-Dispatch. "Three Die in Helicopter Crash." May 28, 1982. https://www.newspapers.com.

Roanoke Times. "Stories to Make You Shiver." October 30, 2004. https://roanoke.com.

Shearer, Kathy. *Working for Stuarts*. Emory, VA: Clinch Mountain Press, 2015.

Spokane (WA) Chronicle. "Spy Trial's Prosecutor Stresses U-2 Flight Plan." August 18, 1960.

Steely, Michael S. *Swift's Silver Mines and Related Appalachian Treasures*. Johnson City, TN: Overmountain Press, 1995.

Tabler, D. "Two of the World's Oldest Family Businesses Are Appalachian." Appalachian History, September 8, 2008. https://www.appalachianhistory.net.

———. "Which of Them Really Invented 'Dr Pepper'?" Appalachian History, July 25, 2018. https://www.appalachianhistory.net.

Taylor, L.B. *The Big Book of Virginia Ghost Stories*. Mechanicsburg, PA: Stackpole Books, 2010.

Veronese, K. "The Weird but True History of Sin-Eaters." Gizmodo, April 30, 2013. https://gizmodo.com.

Viccellio, R. "Did You Know? A Collection of University Esoterica." *UVA Magazine*, Winter 2009. https://uvamagazine.org.

Vickery, Dorothy S. *Mollie Tynes, Civil War Heroine*. Commonwealth, 1938.

Ward, Harry M. "Campbell, William." American National Biography Online, February 2000. https://www.anb.org.

Wigington, P. "Appalachian Folk Magic and Granny Witchcraft." Learn Religions, December 28, 2019. https://www.learnreligions.com.

Williamson, Seth. "Allen Clan Hillsville Courthouse Shootout." *Roanoker Magazine*, November 1982.

Windsor Daily Star (Ontario, CAN). "Text of Judge Picard's Portal-to-Portal Decision." February 10, 1947.

ABOUT THE AUTHORS

Melody Blackwell-West grew up in the beautiful rolling hills of Honaker in Russell County. She was raised surrounded by amazing storytellers who fueled the flames of her passion for local history and folklore. She is a graduate of East Tennessee State University with a degree in Allied Health and has a passion for helping others. When not working, you can find her exploring the winding roads of Real Appalachia with Shane for their YouTube travel vlog. In her spare time, she loves to hike, read, watch movies and spend time with her family and friends. Her perfect day though would be curled up with a cat in her lap, a coffee, a book and a rainy mountain view, surrounded by the ones she loves.

Shane Simmons was born and raised in Tazewell County, where he developed an appreciation for the rich history and heritage of Southwest Virginia. His family was involved in the coal mining industry, which helped instill in him a strong sense of community and brotherhood and inspired him to tell the stories of the people and events that have shaped the area. He graduated

from historic Emory and Henry College in Emory, Virginia, with a degree in business management. In 2016, he wrote his first book, *Legends & Lore of East Tennessee*, which earned him the Award of Distinction given by the East Tennessee Historical Society in 2017. In 2019, he also coauthored a children's book titled *Petey the Pink-Tailed Possum: A School Tale*.

Visit us at
www.historypress.com